NEW DIRECTIONS FOR COMMUNITY COLLEGES

Arthur M. Cohen
EDITOR-IN-CHIEF

Florence B. Brawer
ASSOCIATE EDITOR

Implementing Effective Policies for Remedial and Developmental Education

Jan M. Ignash
Illinois Board of Higher Education

EDITOR

Number 100, Winter 1997

JOSSEY-BASS PUBLISHERS
San Francisco

ERIC®
Clearinghouse for Community Colleges

IMPLEMENTING EFFECTIVE POLICIES FOR REMEDIAL AND DEVELOPMENTAL EDUCATION
Jan M. Ignash (ed.)
New Directions for Community Colleges, no. 100
Volume XXV, number 4
Arthur M. Cohen, Editor-in-Chief
Florence B. Brawer, Associate Editor

New Directions for Community Colleges is indexed in Current Index to Journals in Education (ERIC).

Microfilm copies of issues and articles are available in 16mm and 35mm, as well as microfiche in 105mm, through University Microfilms Inc., 300 North Zeeb Road, Ann Arbor, Michigan 48106-1346.

ISSN 0194-3081   ISBN 0-7879-9843-5

NEW DIRECTIONS FOR COMMUNITY COLLEGES is part of The Jossey-Bass Higher and Adult Education Series and is published quarterly by Jossey-Bass Inc., Publishers, 350 Sansome Street, San Francisco, California 94104-1342, in association with the ERIC Clearinghouse for Community Colleges. Periodicals postage paid at San Francisco, California, and at additional mailing offices. POSTMASTER: Send address changes to New Directions for Community Colleges, Jossey-Bass Inc., Publishers, 350 Sansome Street, San Francisco, California 94104-1342.

SUBSCRIPTIONS cost $55.00 for individuals and $98.00 for institutions, agencies, and libraries. Prices subject to change.

THE MATERIAL in this publication is based on work sponsored wholly or in part by the Office of Educational Research and Improvement, U.S. Department of Education, under contract number RI-93-00-2003. Its contents do not necessarily reflect the views of the Department or any other agency of the U.S. Government.

EDITORIAL CORRESPONDENCE should be sent to the Editor-in-Chief, Arthur M. Cohen, at the ERIC Clearinghouse for Community Colleges, University of California, 3051 Moore Hall, 405 Hilgard Avenue, Los Angeles, California 90024-1521.

Cover photograph © Rene Sheret, After Image, Los Angeles, California, 1990.

Jossey-Bass Web address: http://www.josseybass.com

Printed in the United States of America on acid-free recycled paper containing 100 percent recovered waste paper, of which at least 20 percent is postconsumer waste.

CONTENTS

EDITOR'S NOTES

This issue is devoted to policies about remedial/developmental education. At the time this issue goes to press, national discussions are occurring about the effectiveness of higher education, spurred in part because of the upcoming 1998 reauthorization of the Higher Education Act. The place of remedial/developmental education within higher education is undergoing scrutiny. Much attention is being paid to who needs remedial/developmental education and why, how much it costs, and whether it is effective. Legislators and the public ask why remedial/developmental education is necessary in higher education and are concerned about the perceived devaluation of a college education.

The issue of postsecondary remedial/developmental education is not a simple one and defies quick fixes. Taking the long view, more than 40 percent of college freshmen in 1894 enrolled in pre-collegiate programs to prepare for regular college programs (Levine, 1978, p. 57). This was at a time when only 238,000 students enrolled in all of higher education, a considerably smaller percentage of the U.S. population than the more than fourteen million students enrolled today (USDE, 1996b, pp. 3, 175). A century later, in 1994, 42 percent of high school graduates aged eighteen to twenty-four enrolled in college (USDE, 1996a, p. 54). Today, with a greater percentage of the U.S. population continuing beyond secondary school to higher education, and greater numbers of older students enrolling in higher education, we find that 13 percent of entering freshmen are enrolled in remedial/developmental education (Knopp, 1995, p. 1). But for all the public debate, the percentage of students enrolled in higher education who need remediation may not be as great as perceived, especially in comparison to the 40 percent turn-of-the-century figure. Surely we have come a fair distance.

This is not to say that the problem is not important and difficult to address. Legislators, the public, university administrators, and students, too, are unhappy with the time and expense necessary to remediate English and math skills that should have been learned in high school. While we educate more people than we used to, we are also faced with diminishing resources for higher education. How do we continue to ensure that individuals have the personal and professional opportunities that higher education can provide while at the same time managing our diminishing resources so that we are indeed fair about who has access to higher education? Should we insist that all remediation take place in the high schools? Should students have to pay the full cost of postsecondary remedial instruction after the first attempt, as has been proposed by Florida's legislature? Should community colleges provide all or the bulk of remedial/developmental education? Should students be forced to remediate if they are not ready for college-level classes?

This volume is devoted to a discussion of policies on remedial/developmental education. Hartmark and Hines list four aspects to policy analysis: it involves institutions, it encompasses values and expectations, it sheds light on a public problem, and it can take several forms—description, explanation, criticism, evaluation, or some combination (Hartmark and Hines, 1986).

Each chapter in this volume addresses a specific policy question and fulfills the above criteria. Several chapters in this issue function as case studies and discuss innovative community college policies and programs in dealing with remedial/developmental education. Other chapters discuss state or national policies.

In Chapter One, I describe the current controversy over whether community colleges should provide all, or almost all, remedial/developmental education. The five policy recommendations presented are based on an analysis of the characteristics of students who need remediation and call for universities to assume their share of the responsibility for remediation.

In Chapter Two, Virginia K. McMillan, Scott J. Parke, and Carol A. Lanning identify characteristics of effective remedial/developmental programs, taking into consideration increasing demands for accountability and the pressure to keep pace with technological developments. The authors explore the influence of learning theory on remedial/developmental education programs and draw on the results of applied studies to present a set of policies common to effective remedial/developmental programs.

Both Chapters Three and Four address the policy issue of whether students should be forced to remediate. Dorothy M. Berger presents information from a case study at a large urban community college that instituted a policy of mandatory assessment and placement of students in remedial/developmental math and English classes after having functioned under an open entry/open exit system for many years. The college has also returned to a system in which prerequisites are enforced. Although the process has been complicated by external legal challenges and the difficulty of getting faculty in a large district to agree on standards, the college stayed the course and implemented the changes in fall 1997.

In Chapter Four, Richard Fonte discusses the same issue of whether students should be forced to remediate by presenting another case study from a large suburban community college that underwent a transformation from a "laissez-faire" open access system of remedial/developmental education to a highly structured one. Based on the work of Beatty-Guenter, Fonte describes the fourteen campus policies that constitute its "structured open access" system of responding to the problem of underprepared students. The fourteen policies use mandatory sorting and transforming strategies when students enter the college and active, interventionist connecting and supporting strategies when students enter remedial/developmental classes so that the problems of underprepared students are not ignored.

In Chapter Five, Reuel Kurzet discusses the dilemma of whether to meet the educational demands of a growing number of students or to cap enrollment to answer concerns about program quality. The policy issue she deals with is how much remediation community colleges should provide. Her discussion revolves around English-as-a-second-language students, and although students who enroll in ESL are not necessarily considered enrolled in remedial/developmental coursework, the issue of quantity versus quality is a central policy issue in remedial/developmental education.

In Chapter Six, Deborah K. Richey, Jeanette Mathern, Carol S. O'Shea, and Shelby J. Pierce present a case study of a successful community college/high school feedback project that addresses the issue of how to reduce the need for remediation in writing before students enter college as freshmen. Funded as part of Ohio's Early Warning Program, which was created by the Ohio General Assembly in 1984 and is administered by the Ohio Board of Regents, this project is one of a number of highly successful faculty development and student development ventures.

In Chapter Seven, Julie Weissmann, Carole Bulakowski, and Marci K. Jumisko discuss the use of research to evaluate developmental education. The issue they address is how we know if a college's remedial/developmental program and services are effective in remediating students. With accountability an increasingly important component of higher education, the authors argue that evaluation should go beyond simply determining if courses are effective. Evaluation of remedial/developmental programs should also examine the placement of students, timing of remediation, and eventual student enrollment in college-level courses as measures of effectiveness.

The policy issue of whether financial aid policies restrict access to higher education for at-risk and minority students is addressed by Michael B. Goldstein in Chapter Eight. He explains the variety of federal laws that seek to protect the rights of individuals as well as the integrity of federal funds. And although these interests may come into conflict, problems are manageable and student needs can be met.

The final chapter, by Kristen J. McKinney, is devoted to additional sources of current research, programs, and initiatives that provide information about the policy issues discussed in this volume.

Mention should be made of the use of the term *remedial/developmental* throughout this volume. Although there are real philosophical and methodological differences between the terms *remedial* and *developmental,* this volume mirrors the current and common practice of using the hybrid term *remedial/developmental.* What is lost in this hybrid term is the use of the term *remedial* to refer to programs that focus on providing remedies for specific deficiencies in reading, writing, and math, and use of the term *developmental* to refer to programs that focus on the whole learner, with the unique blend of academic and personal strengths and weaknesses that each individual brings to the learning process. The less frequently used term *compensatory education* is also encompassed in the use of *remedial/developmental* throughout this issue. Debate over the merits of the original meanings of *remedial* and *developmental* is beyond the scope of this volume.

Jan M. Ignash
Editor

References

Levine, A. *Handbook on Undergraduate Curriculum.* San Francisco: Jossey-Bass Publishers, 1978.

Hartmark, L. S., and Hines, E. R. "Politics and Policy in Higher Education: Reflections on the Status of the Field." In S. K. Gove and T. M. Stauffer (eds.), *Policy Controversies in Higher Education.* New York: Greenwood Press, 1986.

Knopp, L. "Remedial Education: An Undergraduate Student Profile." *Research Briefs,* 1995, 6 (entire issue 8).

United States Department of Education, National Center for Education Statistics. *The Condition of Education 1996,* NCES 96–304, by T. M. Smith. Washington, D.C.: U.S. Government Printing Office, 1996a.

U.S. Department of Education. National Center for Education Statistics. *Digest of Education Statistics 1996,* NCES 96–133, by T. D. Snyder, C. M. Hoffman, and C. M. Geddes. Washington, D.C.: U.S. Government Printing Office, 1996b.

JAN M. IGNASH is an assistant director of academic affairs at the Illinois Board of Higher Education.

Current attempts to limit remediation in some states are simplistic. Policies should consider the complexity of remediation in higher education and the differing characteristics of students who need remedial/developmental work.

Who Should Provide Postsecondary Remedial/Developmental Education?

Jan M. Ignash

As resources in higher education have grown tighter in the 1990s, the controversy over who should provide remedial/developmental education in higher education has also grown. Community colleges claim that they deliver a disproportionate amount of remediation and that, as a result, transfer and occupational functions are threatened. Four-year institutions assert that because remediation is not collegiate-level education, they should not be required to provide it. Everyone blames the high schools, but educators there cite crippling handicaps of overcrowded classrooms, poorly funded schools, and a breakdown in support structures for children that militate against their efforts to prepare students for college. Who, then, is responsible for remediation in higher education?

The first part of this chapter discusses the controversy surrounding remedial/developmental education and the attempts in different states to end or limit remediation after high school. Included is discussion of some of the core issues: state policies on remediation, cost, standards, and effectiveness. The second part of this chapter looks at data describing the characteristics of students who need remediation, with an emphasis on the bipolar age distribution of students who take remedial courses, as well as the amount and seriousness of remediation needed. Based on the student characteristics data, the third section addresses the central question of which sector of higher education should

The author would like to thank Andrew Malizio of the National Center for Education Statistics for his assistance in running analyses from the 1992 National Postsecondary Student Aid Survey (NPSAS: 93) that provide the data for Tables 1.1 and 1.2.

be responsible for remedial/developmental education and provides policy recommendations for addressing the problem of remediation in higher education.

The Controversy

Several states and higher education systems have attempted to ban or limit remedial/developmental courses and services, with varying degrees of success. In 1994 about half of the incoming freshmen in the twenty-two-campus California State University (CSU) system needed remedial work in English or math (Kirst, 1997). The Trustees of the CSU system proposed shifting 90 percent of its remedial education to the community colleges by the year 2007, charging that the need to provide so many remedial courses "threaten[ed] the value of a CSU diploma" (Gallego, 1995, p. 3). In the face of strong opposition from community colleges and other groups, the trustees of the CSU system have put the proposed policy on hold, although discussions of what to do about remediation are continuing (Charles McIntyre, Research and Planning, California Community College Chancellor's Office, personal communication, May 21, 1997).

Other efforts to limit remediation have addressed the fact that not just freshmen take remedial courses. In 1995 a committee of the Trustees of the City University of New York considered restricting baccalaureate program admissions to only those students who could complete remedial or English as a second language courses during their freshman year. The measure was one of several that were proposed in reaction to deep budget cuts by both the city and the state ("Ways and Means," 1995, p. A21).

University officials are not the only ones attempting to take action. Legislators, too, have been increasingly involved in the debate over remediation, as seen by proposals in California to charge the high schools, through a deduction in state aid, for part of the cost of university remedial courses (Kirst, 1997). Legislators in Florida have prohibited public universities from providing remedial courses, although Florida's A & M University, a historically black college, is excluded from the legislation and community college faculty are allowed to go to four-year campuses to teach remedial courses (Burd, 1996, p. A38).

Florida's efforts to legislate remediation, however, do not end with the public universities. In 1996 the Florida legislature passed a bill that would limit community college students to two attempts per course in the skill areas of reading, writing, and math, with students required to pay the full cost of instruction, four times greater than the regular tuition rate, after the first attempt. Also mandated were higher cut-off scores in college preparation "bridge" courses. Analyses by staff at Miami-Dade Community College on the effect of these new cut-off scores in the skill area of reading show that 72 percent of entering students would place into college preparatory reading classes—up from 50 percent of entering students under the old cut-off scores. Although the governor has yet to sign this legislation, educators at the college are worried about the potential effect upon student enrollment and access to higher education (Janet Rich, Associate Dean of Institutional Research, Miami-Dade Community College, personal communication, May 22, 1997).

An attempt by the New Jersey Commission on Higher Education to reduce the approximately $50 million annual price tag for remediation proposes that all students enrolling in higher education take a mandatory admissions test to judge each student's level of preparation in reading, writing, math computation, and elementary algebra. "The state's proposal is deliberately vague on whether the assessment could be used as a basis for acceptance to a school" ("N.J. Eyes Remedial Testing," 1996, p. 4).

Calls to limit remediation are not new. And neither is the general belief that public four-year universities and colleges should not be in the business of remediation. Over the past few years attempts have been made to limit remediation in Arkansas, Louisiana, Oklahoma, Tennessee, and Virginia, with officials in Nebraska, Minnesota, and West Virginia also investigating the scope of remediation in higher education (Lively, 1993). The Illinois statute addressing the role of state universities in providing remediation is clear—and not uncommon—among state policies addressing minimum academic standards. The Illinois law states that "the primary emphasis on postsecondary remedial programs [is] at Public Community Colleges" and that "the role of the state universities in offering remedial programs should be reduced" (110 ILCS, 205/9.07(c)).

Perhaps the public's greatest concern in the debate about who should provide remediation is cost. Legislators and the public are upset over the perception that they are paying twice for the same education: once in high school and once again in college. In Texas, $155 million was spent on postsecondary remediation in 1996 (McMillan, 1997). Louisiana spent $32 million in 1992–93 (Lively, 1993). New Jersey estimates that it spends $50 million a year on postsecondary remediation ("N.J. Eyes Remedial Testing," 1996, p. 4). In Oklahoma the cost of remedial courses was $18.7 million in 1991–92 (Oklahoma State Regents for Higher Education, 1993).

Media coverage that reports costs for remediation outside the context of all instructional costs, however, is misleading. A recent cooperative study by the Illinois Board of Higher Education and the Illinois Community College Board reported $27 million devoted to direct faculty instructional costs (excluding support staff, equipment, and other indirect costs) for all remedial/developmental courses for fiscal year 1996. This large amount, however, must be set in the context of direct faculty instructional costs for all of Illinois public higher education during fiscal year 1996, which was $672 million—$313 million for universities and $359 million for community colleges (Illinois Board of Higher Education, 1997, p. 7). For public universities, $3.4 million, or just over 1 percent of direct faculty salary costs, was devoted to remediation; for public community colleges, the figure was $23.4 million, or 6.5 percent. Part of the difficulty in attempting to assess all costs involved in remedial/developmental education lies in the fact that institutions use different measures to report indirect costs.

Public and private universities are understandably upset about the extent and cost of remediation. They are also concerned about the potential loss of status when universities provide an undue amount of remediation. Some educators believe that community colleges should provide remediation because of their emphasis on teaching and learning and the lower cost of instruction. The following university catalog description is illustrative of this thinking: "While the university offers a wide range of support services to improve students' chances for academic success, it does not offer remedial assistance in mathematics, reading or composition. Students who believe that they have deficiencies in these basic skills are advised to enroll in appropriate preparatory courses elsewhere before enrolling" (Illinois State University, Undergraduate Catalog 1997–98, p. 9).

Community colleges provide the bulk of postsecondary remediation, followed by public four-year institutions and then by private two- and four-year colleges and universities. The fall 1995 National Center for Education Statistics (NCES) survey of 3,060 two- and four-year college campuses in the United States and Puerto Rico reported that 100 percent of public two-year and 80 percent of public four-year institutions that enroll freshmen offered remedial courses. In the private sector, approximately two-thirds (63 percent) of the two- and four-year colleges offered remedial courses (USDE, 1996d, p. 6).

But as the demand for remediation increases and the resources for education diminish, both universities and community colleges are less and less inclined to accept responsibility for postsecondary remediation. And calls from four-year institutions for community colleges to assume a greater proportion of postsecondary education are increasingly being resisted. In the words of the chancellor of one of the largest urban community college districts in the country, "We must not destroy the integrity of the ongoing occupational and academic programs serving so many of our community college students by just shifting existing resources to remedial work" (Gallego, 1995).

The fall 1995 NCES study also found that state policies tended to designate community colleges as the preferred provider of remediation. State policies discouraged or restricted remedial education at 29 percent of public four-year institutions, but at only 5 percent of public two-year institutions. Ninety percent of two-year institutions also reported that their state policies required or encouraged them to offer remediation, compared to only 59 percent of four-year institutions (USDE, 1996d, p. 29).

Four-year institutions themselves, rather than state agencies or legislatures, tended to limit how much remediation was offered. Ninety-four percent of four-year public and 98 percent of four-year private institutions set their own time limits on remediation. For the community colleges, however, 41 percent of responding institutions reported that they set time limits on remediation, compared to 53 percent with limits set through state policies or laws (USDE, 1996d, p. 30).

The question, then, is who should provide remedial and developmental education to students in higher education? Which sector should assume responsibility?

Developing the Solution

It is not possible to answer the question of which sector of higher education should be responsible for remediation without looking at who needs remediation after high school and how much, and whether this need will continue at the same level in the future. The age, race and ethnicity, and home language of the student, whether the student dropped out of high school or completed an alternative credential like the General Educational Developmental certificate, and whether the student needs additional work in reading or math and at what level all bear on the question of which sector of higher education should provide remedial/developmental education and how much.

Current and Projected Demand for Postsecondary Remediation. Estimates vary, but the number of students remediating is substantial by anyone's count. The fall 1995 NCES study reported that 29 percent of entering, first-time freshmen at public and private two- and four-year institutions took at least one remedial reading, writing, or mathematics course. For public community colleges alone, the figure was 41 percent. For public four-year colleges and universities, 22 percent of entering first-time freshmen took a remedial course (USDE, 1996d, p. 6). That percentage has not changed since fall 1989, the last time that NCES collected these data (USDE, 1991, p. 26).

Regarding the percentage of courses, the Center for the Study of Community Colleges' 1991 curriculum study reported that 30 percent of all English courses and 16 percent of all math courses in two-year institutions were remedial. These tallies did not include non-course-based remediation available through self-paced, individualized, or laboratory courses in math and English (Cohen and Ignash, 1993, p. 15).

Freshmen are not the only students, however, who take remedial courses, although they constitute the largest class. Using NCES data, Knopp found that although the majority of students enrolled in remedial courses were freshmen (56 percent), 24 percent of remedial course-takers were sophomores, 9 percent were juniors, and 9 percent were seniors (1995, p. 3). Graduate students may also need refresher math or writing courses, especially if several years have passed since they earned their bachelor's degrees or if they enroll in a graduate field that demands greater proficiency in these skills than required in their undergraduate degree programs.

As college enrollment rises, educators can expect that there will be an increased demand for remedial/developmental courses, if not in terms of percentages of total student enrollment, then at least in terms of numbers of students needing remediation. A "middle alternative projection" by the U.S. Department of Education predicts that college enrollment will increase by 16 percent over the next ten years, although that prediction varies by region (USDE, 1996c, p. 11). Forty-six states are expected to experience a 15 percent increase in the number of high school graduates between 1993–94 and 2005–06, with a 33 percent increase in Western states (USDE, 1996c, p. 115). If no improvements are made in preparing high school students academically for college and all other conditions remain static, then one could expect that 16 percent of this increased pool of students will also take at least one remedial course, creating an increase in the real numbers of students who will need remediation in the year 2006.

Age. U.S. Census data show that most college students enroll in college immediately after completing high school. In 1994, 62 percent of high school graduates went directly to college, up from 47 percent in 1973. Of the 62 percent who enrolled in 1994, 41 percent went to four-year colleges and universities and 21 percent went to two-year colleges (USDE, 1996a, p. 52).

The population that needs remediation, however, can be thought of as bipolar in terms of age and time elapsed between secondary and postsecondary educational experiences. If 62 percent of high school graduates go directly to college, what of the nearly 40 percent who do not? A considerable number of high school graduates find jobs, enter the military, begin raising families, or pursue other avenues that may delay their entry into further education.

Table 1.1 lists the age of entering, first-year undergraduate students who took at least one remedial course in 1992–93 and provides evidence that the remedial/developmental student population may indeed be bipolar. As the table shows, less than one-third (30.6 percent) of entering freshmen who took a remedial class in 1992–93 were nineteen years old or younger. Although not everyone graduates from high school at age eighteen, the data suggest that close to half of the proportion of students who enroll in remedial courses are at least several years away from the high school experience. The data show that a little less than half (45.3 percent) of the entering freshmen who took a remedial course were over twenty-two years of age, the traditional age of baccalaureate degree graduation. These students, then, are already four or five years beyond the traditional age of high school graduation.

These data are corroborated in a recent report by the Institute for Higher Education Policy in Washington, D.C., and The Education Resources Institute (TERI) in Boston, which reported that between 1970 and 1993 the participation in higher education by students forty years of age and over increased from 5.5 percent of total enrollment in higher education to 11.2 percent, "the largest jump of any age cohort" (*Life After Forty,* 1996, p. 15). The report warns that an increase in the older, nontraditional student, along with a concomitant increase in the "echo boom" generation of college-goers, could have serious consequences for staff and facility needs in higher education and could threaten to overwhelm existing educational infrastructures (p. 18).

For policy purposes, the difference in age groups of students who take remedial/developmental courses is an important one. Legislators and the public more easily accept the fact that an older, returning student needs a refresher math or writing class than the fact that a student who enters college right out of high school is unprepared for college-level coursework. It is important for legislators and the public to know that the increase in the demand for remediation is being fueled in part by older students who are returning to college. Differences in program structure for these two groups of students will be discussed later in this chapter.

Table 1.1. Age of Students Who Took a Remedial Class During 1992–93

Age of Entering Freshmen (Years)	Percentage of Students Who Took at Least One Remedial Course in 1992–93
18 and under	15.09 %
19	15.51
20	10.25
21	6.91
22	6.45
Subtotal, 22 and under:	54.21
23	3.75
24	2.84
25–29	12.60
30–34	10.11
35–39	7.63
40–49	7.19
50–59	1.40
60 and over	0.27
Subtotal, 23 and over:	45.79

Source: National Center for Education Statistics, NPSAS 93 Survey, unpublished tabulations, May 1997.

Race/Ethnicity.   Race/ethnicity is an important characteristic to consider in developing higher education policies on remedial/developmental education. Table 1.2 provides an illustration of participation rates in remedial/developmental education by racial/ethnic group in proportion to their overall representation in higher education.

The fall 1995 NCES study on remedial education reported that more remedial/developmental courses were offered by institutions having high minority enrollment and that the extent of remediation was often linked to open admissions policies. Only 15 percent of institutions with low minority enrollment had open admissions policies, compared to about a third of all institutions with high minority enrollment (USDE, 1996d, p. 6).

Differences between racial and ethnic groups were also found in the type of remedial classes taken. As the NCES data reported in Table 1.3 indicate, of first-year undergraduate students in 1993 who took at least one remedial/developmental course, Hispanic and Asian/Pacific Islander students took more remedial reading and writing courses than African-American or white students, who enrolled in more remedial math courses.

The results also suggest that more Hispanic and Asian-American students were enrolled in English as a second language courses to improve English language proficiency, as discussed below.

Somewhat different results, however, were reported from research that limited the pool of subjects to students who had attended at least one four-year institution and who had earned more than a semester's worth of credits by the time they were thirty years of age. Using transcript data from the high school

Table 1.2. Participation in Remedial/Developmental Education by Racial/Ethnic Group

Race/Ethnicity	Percentage Enrolled in Higher Education, Fall 1992[a]	Percentage Taking at Least One Remedial Class, 1992–93
African American	10 %	19 %
Asian American	5	19
Hispanic	7	19
Native American	1	15
White	75	11
Alien	3	—

[a]Because of rounding, column does not sum to 100 percent.

Source: Knopp, 1995, p. 2.

graduating classes of 1972 and 1982, Adelman (1996) reported shifts in the population of students who took remedial reading based on race/ethnicity and gender. Higher percentages of African-American male and female students and Latino male students, in particular, enrolled in more remedial reading classes between 1972 and 1982, compared to white students and Latino female students. Adelman suggested that remedial reading participation rates were a strong factor in degree completion and concluded that "deficiencies in reading skills are indicators of comprehensive literacy problems" and "we cannot continue to let high-school graduates believe that they have a good chance of earning a college degree if they leave high school with poor reading skills" (p. A56).

The fact that minority students not only take more remedial classes but also take more remedial reading classes has serious implications for their persistence and completion rates in higher education.

Extent of Remediation. How much remediation a student needs is also a factor in developing effective policies on remedial/developmental education. Studies have shown that there is a difference in the persistence and success rates of students who need one remedial course in math or English compared to students who need three or four remedial courses. The population of students needing remediation may be bipolar not only in terms of age and distance from the secondary experience but also in terms of the amount of remediation required. (See Chapter Seven of this issue for a discussion of the differential achievement of students who take one or several remedial courses.)

Special analysis of data from the High School and Beyond Study (Class of 1982) revealed that, of students who earned more than ten credits by the time they were thirty years old, only 8 percent who took more than four remedial courses and 13 percent who took three or four remedial courses earned an associate's or bachelor's degree by 1993. For students who did not take a remedial course, 43.5 percent earned a degree by the time they were thirty. Adelman states that "the extent of a student's need for remediation is inversely related to his or her eventual completion of a degree" (1996, p. A56).

Table 1.3. Of All Students Taking a Remedial Course During 1992–93, the Percentage Taking Specific Subjects

Race/Ethnicity	Remedial Math	Remedial Reading	Remedial Writing
African American	64.9	44.7	38.0[a]
Asian/Pacific Islander	35.3	78.7	74.7
Hispanic	55.9	57.6	52.6
White	64.7	39.5	30.8

[a]Rows total more than 100 percent because, within each racial/ethnic group, a student could take more than one remedial subject.

Source: National Center for Education Statistics, NPSAS 93 Survey, unpublished tabulations, May 1997.

How much remediation students need changes, too, as the level of knowledge in a field changes or skills required to do a job become more specialized. In the past few years, some states have raised the bar on what is considered remediation in math, in an effort to improve standards and send a clearer message to secondary school students and educators about standards for success in college. Students who do not have college-level proficiency in math, for example, will find it difficult to succeed in math-intensive majors in many of the computer science, engineering, health care, and technical fields. In fall 1993 all Illinois public universities and colleges reclassified Intermediate Algebra from collegiate-level to developmental-level coursework. One effect of this change was to more than double the number of remedial credit hours offered at Illinois community colleges between fiscal year 1991 and fiscal year 1996 (Illinois Board of Higher Education, 1997. p. 5). At the 1997 conference of the American Association of Community Colleges, keynote speaker Representative Howard McKeon, a principal member of the committee on the 1998 reauthorization of the Higher Education Act, noted that we have raised the bar on what remedial is from twenty years ago and that math competencies and other basic skills requirements may continue to change as we expect students to do more technologically sophisticated jobs in the future (McKeon, 1997).

English as a Second Language. In assessing who needs remediation and whether the need will continue at the same level, colleges and universities also need to consider the special needs of ESL populations for additional instruction in reading and writing skills. In a *Wall Street Journal* article, Melinda Beck reported that "approximately 15 percent of U.S. births in recent years were to foreign-born mothers, with origins so diverse that more than 100 different languages are spoken in the school systems of New York City, Chicago, Los Angeles, and Fairfax County, Va." (1997, p. B1).

Projections to the year 2006 predict that Hispanic Americans and Asian Americans will be the fastest growing segments of the U.S. population and that much of this increase will occur through immigration (Hodgkinson, 1996, p. 8). Many will speak English as their home language or be fully bilingual, but some will also need instruction in English. The U.S. Census Bureau estimated in 1990 that approximately 3 percent of all U.S. households, or 5,764,600 persons, spoke English "not well" or "not at all"—an increase from 2 percent reported in the 1980 Census (Ignash, 1994, p. 7)). Additional data show that 21 percent of students whose home language is not English take a postsecondary level remedial/developmental course, compared to 10 percent of those whose primary language is English (Knopp, 1995, pp. 6–8).

As reported elsewhere (see Ignash, 1994, pp. 31–35), whether ESL is considered remedial education is hotly debated. Proponents of ESL argue that ESL students are not cognitively deficient and ESL should be considered akin to a foreign language, while opponents argue that ESL courses do not contain college-level material and are therefore analogous to remedial/developmental education. The level of ESL often determines whether it is considered remedial or collegiate-level education, with advanced ESL writing often considered equivalent to regular college-level freshman composition. The 1995 NCES study of remedial education reported that of the 47 percent of institutions that enrolled freshmen and offered ESL courses, 38 percent considered all of their ESL courses to be remedial, 24 percent considered some of their ESL courses to be remedial, and 38 percent considered none of their ESL courses to be remedial (USDE, 1996d, p. 25).

The differences by sector are marked, however. Fifty-five percent of public two-year colleges considered all of their ESL courses to be remedial, and only 15 percent reported that none of their ESL classes were remedial. For public four-year institutions, however, 35 percent declared all their ESL classes were remedial and 48 percent said none of them were (USDE, 1996d, p. 25). Educators at four-year institutions claim the type of remedial/developmental and ESL education they provide is at a higher level than that of community colleges

Drop-Out Rates and GED Completion Rates. Other student performance characteristics that inform the debate about who should provide remediation are drop-out rates and General Educational Development (GED) completion rates. U.S. Census Bureau studies distinguish between *event* drop-out rates and *status* drop-out rates. Both are important for colleges and universities to note. Event drop-out rates refer to the percentage of students in grades 10 through 12 who drop out in a single year. Status drop-out rates refer to the total percentage of students aged eighteen to twenty-four who dropped out of high school, did not complete a GED, and did not enroll in any further education. U.S. census data indicate that the status drop-out rate for persons sixteen to twenty-four years old in 1995 was 12 percent (USDE, 1996b, p. 110). It is important to note that the status drop-out rates are substantially higher for minority students. Whereas 8.6 percent of white, non-Hispanic persons aged sixteen to twenty-four dropped out of high school, the figures rise to 12.1 percent for Black, non-Hispanic students and 30 percent for students of Hispanic origin.

GED preparation courses can help test-takers prepare themselves for the examination, and some who successfully pass may not require remediation if they go on for further education. But only one-third of those who complete an alternative high school credential enroll in further education, and some research shows that GED recipients are not as successful in further education as those who complete the high school diploma (USDE, 1996b, pp. 27–28). (See also Quinn and Haberman, 1986; Cameron and Heckman, 1993.)

What this means for colleges and universities is that GED completers may need additional assistance before beginning collegiate-level programs and that colleges that admit students with GED or other alternative credentials should ensure that appropriate counseling and academic services are available.

Who Should Provide Remediation: Toward Good Policy

To return to our central question—Who should provide remedial/developmental education?—the short answer is that everyone should. The longer answer is that community colleges have a greater role in addressing existing needs for remediation, whereas public universities, especially those with strong teacher education programs, have a greater role in reducing the need for future remediation.

Because community colleges are more accessible to students in terms of cost, location, and admissions policies, they will always provide more remediation than four-year institutions. And they should. Community colleges are in a better position to provide instruction to students who have the more serious lack of reading skills because they generally have more faculty and support staff with specialty degrees and experience in the field of reading, a subject that cannot be taught by merely anyone who knows how to read.

But in light of the preceding discussion concerning the disproportionate representation of minority students in remedial/developmental education, four-year institutions cannot shirk their responsibilities in assuring equity in higher education by banning or severely limiting remediation on their campuses. The fact that minority students have historically taken not only more remedial classes but also more remedial *reading* classes has serious implications for their retention and persistence in higher education. Both two- and four-year institutions need to track course-taking patterns with persistence and completion rates by gender and race/ethnicity. In addition, public university teacher education programs have a role to play in addressing remediation by providing future teachers in middle schools and junior and senior high schools with the knowledge and skills to recognize and effectively address the problems of students who lack basic skills for college.

Policies on student preparation, access, and retention can be crafted to raise standards while also ensuring access to higher education. The policies of the Illinois Board of Higher Education affirm the obligation of all sectors of higher education to provide admitted students with the academic support services needed to maximize the opportunity to succeed. Current policies recommend links between high schools, community colleges, and four-year institutions to provide useful feedback on high school graduates' preparation for college. Other policies adopted in Illinois to address existing needs and reduce the future need to provide remediation include recommendations that colleges and universities inform potential students and their parents about adequate preparation for college, establish special admissions programs for educationally disadvantaged students and for those who did not have the opportunity to complete a college-prep curriculum in high school, assess the academic skills of all entering students, and provide remedial coursework as needed (Illinois Board of Higher Education, 1997, p. 3).

Perhaps the most notable of all of the findings of the NCES studies on remediation emerges from a 1989 report indicating that 40 percent of all institutions offering remediation were not engaged in any activities to decrease the need for it (USDE, 1991, p. 15). Educators need to first inform themselves about the particular characteristics of students who need remedial/developmental education at their institutions and then develop effective programs to address these needs for remediation based upon these characteristics. If four-year colleges and universities admit students who need remedial/developmental education, they have a responsibility to provide the tools to succeed. Policies at four-year institutions that would push all or most of the burden of remediation to the community colleges are wrong-headed and short-sighted, especially in terms of access.

The foregoing discussion on the different characteristics of students who need remedial/developmental education forms the basis for the following five policy recommendations for both two- and four-year institutions:

First, institutions should chart the age distribution of their remedial/developmental student population to determine what proportion are entering directly from high school and what proportion have been out of school for a number of years. Institutions with large transfer student populations should also document the need for remedial/developmental education in this portion of the entering student body and provide feedback to the sending institutions. Institutions should also divide transfer student populations into groups with few credits (twelve or less) and those with greater numbers of transfer credit hours. Feedback to sending institutions that have had a chance to put their stamp on their students can be useful. But feedback to sending institutions when students have taken only a few courses can provide an inaccurate picture of students' levels of performance.

In addition to charting the age distribution of entering students, institutions should gather local or regional census data on the "highest level of education attained by persons age 18 or over, by age, sex, and race/ethnicity" to track the proportion of students in different groups who return for further education. Other useful information includes the numbers of high school students in feeder districts and schools; the numbers of local or regional residents who do not speak English as their home language; area drop-out and GED completion rates, with projections that allow for one-third of GED recipients to enroll in further education and that allow for the likelihood that such students will require more academic support than high school completers; and standardized test scores of local or regional students to indicate the amount and type of remediation students may be expected to need. Furthermore, institutions may need to identify which students can benefit most from remediation and then target remedial resources where they will do the most good, taking care to ensure alignment with institutional mission.

Second, institutions should investigate the use of different methodologies and teaching strategies for remedial/developmental education for students in different age groups. Colleges and universities that admit substantial numbers of nontraditional students should investigate offering specially developed programs and services for returning adults who simply need several weeks of intensive review of math fundamentals or expository writing, like the special "refresher workshops" run by Prairie State College in Chicago Heights, Illinois. The college offers workshops for returning students, as well as workshops especially for returning women, before students take the college's entry assessment tests. In analyzing trends among students who needed remediation, the college discovered that students who had been out of high school for several years or more often tested lower than their real proficiency levels in math and English, but caught up quickly after several weeks back in the classroom (Sheila Lewis, Assistant Dean of Occupational and Technical Education, personal communication, May 27, 1997). Older students may be more mature and motivated more by specific career or personal goals than younger students and may do well in accelerated remedial/developmental courses or combined courses that bridge remedial/developmental and collegiate-level work. This allows students to spend several weeks of intensive review before or during the start of the regular semester to brush up on vocabulary and concepts in math and English that they learned years earlier but have forgotten.

In order to reduce the need for remediation among younger students in the bipolar distribution of students who need remediation, colleges and universities need to develop effective feedback systems with high schools. Several states have made progress in reducing the need for remediation by students who enter directly from high school. State-funded collaborative high school–college programs, like the one described in Chapter Six between Findlay High School and Owens Community College, can make measurable gains in reducing the need for remediation. The Ohio Board of Regents began the Early English Composition Assessment Program writing project in 1984 after its creation by the Ohio General Assembly, and, to date, has funded fifty local community colleges and four-year universities to form collaborative projects with high school faculty that work toward improving classroom practices. Colleges and universities are awarded up to $30,000 in grant funds to identify student writing strengths and weaknesses in relation to the standard expected of college freshman English and to provide high school seniors with the appropriate assistance to meet this standard (H. Marlene Rushay, personal communication, May 21, 1997).

Several states have developed high school feedback systems in which colleges and universities report back to high schools on the freshman year achievement of their students. The Illinois High School Feedback System requires the ten public universities that admit freshmen to collect the following information: ACT composite scores; the self-reported number of years of English, math, and science completed in high school for each entering freshman; freshman English, math, and science course placement level (remedial, regular, or advanced); and grades earned in those subjects during the freshman year of college. The board's policies also encourage colleges and universities to use the data to work cooperatively with high schools to strengthen the preparation of students for college (Illinois Board of Higher Education, 1996). Feedback systems between high schools and postsecondary institutions are currently being reviewed, however, in light of the new Learning Standards developed by the Illinois State Board of Education (K–12 board) that define specific knowledge and skills for all elementary and secondary students in seven fundamental areas: language arts, mathematics, science, social science, physical development and health, fine arts, and foreign languages. As the new standards are implemented, the higher education system in Illinois is expected to work with the Illinois State Board of Education to build college admission standards into the new Illinois Learning Standards. Four-year colleges and universities will also be expected to assist future teachers to teach the knowledge and skills called for in the new Learning Standards (Illinois Board of Higher Education, 1997, pp. 3–4, 23).

In Oklahoma, the State Regents for Higher Education claim a reduction in the need for remediation by both entering freshmen and transfer students as a result of a series of policies begun in spring 1993. The new policies include strengthening college and university admission standards; increasing the number of courses required for college entry; providing high schools, parents, and students with a list of the knowledge and skills students should acquire in the fifteen courses required for college entry; implementing a feedback system that informs parents, principals, and teachers about students' success in college; and publishing brochures on admission and course requirements and placement policies for every eighth through twelfth grade student in Oklahoma (Oklahoma State Regents for Higher Education, 1997).

The third recommendation is for institutions to keep track of how well they are providing effective remediation to disadvantaged minority populations—and that means measuring persistence and achievement. In their book *Meaningful Differences*, Hart and Risley (1995) note that it is false advertising to use median traces and smoothing effects to lump all groups together to report results. It is important that the public know not just how *all* students are doing, but how each group is doing, broken out by race and ethnicity.

Fourth, colleges and universities should specify how much remediation they can realistically provide, based on their mission and the characteristics of both the existing student body and future students. Institutions may have to make tough choices and weigh considerations about the quality of their remedial/developmental education programs against the quantity of students they can enroll in these programs, as discussed by Kurzet in Chapter Five of this volume.

And fifth, state coordinating agencies need to review policies on remedial/developmental education with an eye toward the collective performance of the state's two- and four-year institutions in order to not only maintain standards but also ensure equity for disadvantaged minority students. Policies on remedial/developmental education should not unintentionally establish barriers to full participation in higher education by underrepresented minority populations. All public institutions, and especially four-year colleges and universities, should be encouraged to acknowledge their responsibilities to educate all those who can benefit from higher education.

Conclusion

If nothing changes, we can expect the percentage of the college-age population that needs remedial/developmental education to increase. Part of the reason the problem of postsecondary level remediation seems so intractable is that it is not a simple problem. We are not dealing with a homogeneous population of high school seniors who go on to college without the necessary English and math skills to succeed. Rather, the population can be considered as bipolar both in age, with older students having different needs for remediation than younger students, and in the extent of remediation needed, whether just one class in writing or mathematics is necessary or whether students need three or more remedial/developmental classes. We know considerably more than we used to about the characteristics of students who take remedial/developmental education. Both two-year and four-year colleges and universities can use this information to form appropriate and effective policies to assume their responsibilities in helping students achieve success in higher education.

References

Adelman, C. "The Truth About Remedial Work: It's More Complex Than Windy Rhetoric and Simple Solutions Suggest." *The Chronicle of Higher Education*, Oct. 4, 1996, p. A56.

Beck, M. "Next Population Bulge Shows Its Might." *The Wall Street Journal*, Feb. 3, 1997, pp. B1, B6.

Burd, S. "Colleges Fear Lawmakers Will Cut Funds for Remedial Students." *The Chronicle of Higher Education*, Apr. 12, 1996, pp. A38–A39.

Cameron, S. V., and Heckman, J. J. "The Non-Equivalence of High School Equivalents." *Journal of Labor Economics*, 1993, 11 (1), 1–47.

Cohen, A. M., and Ignash, J. M. *Probing the Community College Transfer Function*. Washington, D.C.: American Council on Education, 1993.

Gallego, A. P. "Another Look at the Remedial Role." *Community College Times*, 1995, 7 (17), 3.

Hart, B., and Risely, T. R. *Meaningful Differences*. Baltimore: Brookes Publishers, 1995.

Hodgkinson, H. L. *Bringing Tomorrow into Focus: Demographic Insights into the Future*. Washington, D.C.: Institute for Educational Leadership, 1996.

Ignash, J. M. "The Scope and Status of English as a Second Language in U.S. Community Colleges." Unpublished doctoral dissertation, University of California at Los Angeles, 1994.

Illinois Board of Higher Education. *Student Preparation for College*. Springfield: Illinois Board of Higher Education, 1996.

Illinois Board of Higher Education. *The Scope and Effectiveness of Remedial/Developmental Education in Illinois Public Universities and Community Colleges*. Springfield: Illinois Board of Higher Education, Sept. 1997.

Kirst, M. "Exam Confusion." *Crosstalk*, 1997, 5 (1), 3.

Knopp, L. *Remedial Education: An Undergraduate Student Profile*. Research Briefs, vol. 6, no. 8. Washington, D.C.: American Council on Education, 1995.

Life After 40: A New Portrait of Today's—and Tomorrow's—Postsecondary Students. Boston: The Education Resources Institute and The Institute for Higher Education Policy, 1996.

Lively, K. "States Try to End Remedial Courses at 4-Year Colleges." *The Chronicle of Higher Education*, Feb. 24, 1993, p. A28.

McKeon, H. "The Higher Education Act Reauthorization: More or Less Opportunity for Community College Students?" Plenary Session at the 77th Annual Convention of the American Association of Community Colleges, Anaheim, California, Apr. 14, 1997.

McMillan, J. "Remedial Education Program in Texas Faces Uncertain Future." *The Chronicle of Higher Education*, Jan. 17, 1997, p. A35.

"N.J. Eyes Remedial Testing for Some College-Bound Students." *Education Daily*, Apr. 10, 1996, p. 4. (Published by Capitol Publications, Inc., Alexandria, Va.)

Oklahoma State Regents for Higher Education. "State Regents Approve Three-Point Plan to Better Prepare Students for College." *Leader,* July 1993, p. 2.

Oklahoma State Regents for Higher Education. "Fewer College Freshmen Need Remedial Courses, Study Shows." *Leader,* Mar. 1997.

Quinn, L., and Haberman, M. "Are GED Certificate Holders Ready for Postsecondary Education?" *Metropolitan Education,* 1986, 2, 27–82.

U.S. Department of Education, National Center for Education Statistics. *College-Level Remedial Education in the Fall of 1989*, NCES 91–191, by W. Mansfield, E. Farris, and M. Black. Washington, D.C.: U.S. Government Printing Office, 1991.

U.S. Department of Education, National Center for Education Statistics. *The Condition of Education, 1996*, NCES 96–304, by T. M. Smith. Washington, D.C.: U.S. Government Printing Office, 1996a.

U.S. Department of Education, National Center for Education Statistics. *Dropout Rates in the United States: 1994*, NCES 96–863, by M. M. McMillen and P. Kaufman. Washington, D.C.: U.S. Government Printing Office, 1996b.

U.S. Department of Education, National Center for Education Statistics. *Projections of Education Statistics to 2006*, NCES 96–661, by W. J. Hussar and D. E. Gerald. Washington, D.C.: U.S. Government Printing Office, 1996c.

U.S. Department of Education, National Center for Education Statistics. *Remedial Education at Higher Education Institutions in Fall 1995*, NCES 97–584, by L. Lewis and E. Farris. Washington, D.C.: U.S. Government Printing Office, 1996d.

"Ways and Means." *The Chronicle of Higher Education*, June 23, 1995, p. A21.

JAN M. IGNASH is an assistant director of academic affairs at the Illinois Board of Higher Education.

This chapter examines remedial/developmental education in the context of an education environment facing new demands and adapting to rapid advances in technology. Rationales for different delivery models for remedial/developmental education are also discussed.

Remedial/Developmental Education Approaches for the Current Community College Environment

Virginia K. McMillan, Scott J. Parke, Carol A. Lanning

The National Center for Educational Statistics (NCES) has defined remedial/developmental education as "courses in reading, writing, or mathematics for college students lacking those skills necessary to perform college-level work at the level required by the institution" (USDE, 1996, p. 2). In an era when publicly funded entities are being held increasingly accountable for student outcomes, the need for high school graduates to strengthen their fundamental academic skills before they are ready for college-level coursework is receiving closer scrutiny. Questions about why additional tax dollars should be spent teaching students skills that they are expected to acquire in high school are being asked with a greater sense of urgency. Adding to the complexity of the issue is the fact that a broad cross section of the population is served by community colleges—including recent high school graduates as well as students who have been out of high school for many years.

As access to higher education has increased, the number of students who require remediation and the amount of public resources spent in providing remediation have grown to alarming proportions. An NCES report recently released by the U.S. Department of Education (1996) found that nationwide, all community colleges surveyed offer remedial/developmental education, and approximately four out of every ten first-time freshmen are underprepared in at least one of the basic skills areas. Statewide studies conducted in Florida, Texas, Maryland, Illinois, and Minnesota, as well as a regional study conducted by the Southern Regional Education Board, reflect similar remedial/developmental course offerings and enrollment patterns (Illinois Community College Board, 1997; Maryland Higher Education Commission,

1996; Reyes, 1996; Schoenecker, Bollman, and Evens, 1996; Ansley, 1991; and Steinberg, 1996).

The scope of remedial/developmental education has grown to the extent that a recent article in *Community College Week* (January 13, 1997, p. 11) likened it to "the education world's equivalent of the elephant-in-the-living-room syndrome: An enormous problem staring you in the face that everyone can see but no one likes to talk about." However unpleasant it may be to acknowledge this "elephant," given the growing public price tag, it is not surprising that debate about remedial/developmental education among educators, legislators, and others has intensified. Policymakers have questioned whether it is appropriate for colleges and universities to offer coursework that is essentially precollegiate. Questions have also been raised regarding who should be responsible for delivering (and paying for) remedial/developmental education. States have considered policies or laws to address the issue that include (1) concentrating remediation in community colleges, (2) limiting remedial/developmental coursework to the freshman year, (3) limiting the number of remedial/developmental courses offered, (4) requiring public school systems to reimburse colleges for remedial/developmental work needed by their graduates, and (5) prohibiting the use of state money to pay for remedial/developmental coursework (USDE, 1996).

Although the need to contain costs for remedial/developmental education is evident, the need for a workforce with solid academic skills is also apparent. McCabe (1996b, p. 4) emphasizes the importance of remedial/developmental education in helping students strengthen their basic academic skills, which are the fundamental skills necessary for employment—"the ability to read, write, analyze, interpret and communicate information are essential skills." Drucker (1994) indicates that the labor market is being transformed and job opportunities will be most plentiful for "knowledge workers." Hence, helping students develop their basic academic skills is an important first step to expanding opportunities for success in the information age.

The need to provide remedial/developmental education programs is pervasive throughout higher education. Nationwide, data from the NCES indicate that across institutional types and levels, 29 percent of first-time freshmen enrolled in at least one remedial/developmental writing, reading, or mathematics course in fall 1995 (USDE, 1996, p. 10). Fifty-five percent of the public two-year colleges reported an increase in remedial/developmental activity over the past five years, compared to 39 percent across all institutional types. Only 5 percent of the two-year public institutions perceived a decrease in the number of remedial/developmental students, compared to 14 percent across all types of institutions (USDE, 1996, p. 11).

The debate regarding the problem of underprepared students and the need for remedial/developmental education in the nation's colleges and universities will undoubtedly continue. Issues of academic excellence and cost to the public need to be balanced with issues of access and student and societal benefits derived from remedial/developmental instruction. In the meantime, institutions of higher education continue to offer remedial/developmental instruction appropriate to their admission policies. For selective institutions, it may be a matter of choice. For institutions with open admissions policies, providing remedial/developmental coursework is a necessity.

Current Environment

Changes in the overall environment surrounding higher education are contributing to the climate outlined above regarding remedial/developmental education. Heightened scrutiny from elected officials increasing their focus on higher education and acting to impose the kinds of additional oversight, accountability, and discipline that other providers of public goods and services have come to accept is a contributing factor to an accelerated change in the environment. Corresponding to a general diminishing respect for major societal institutions, the reverence people hold for institutions of higher education and professors is eroding (Finn, 1997, p. 15). Along with this increased emphasis on accountability comes the increased pressure to keep pace with technological advancement. New instructional tools improve the learning process while at the same time putting additional pressure on the student to develop the requisite skills to perform in today's society. These two key factors will be examined in light of their impact on remedial/developmental education.

Demands for Increased Accountability. Ruppert (1994, p. 1) notes an intensified push for accountability over the past decade, precipitated in most states by "decreases in state resources for higher education, rising costs, and growing demands for access." She goes on to note that the interests of state policy makers are "not only in educational quality but in productivity, efficiency, equity, and effectiveness" (p. 4). Any activity in higher education that appears to require the public to pay twice for the same service invites public scrutiny by policy makers, whether the topic is remedial/developmental education or credits lost by transfer students (those not applicable to a baccalaureate degree) who advance from community colleges to four-year institutions. Ewell (1990) refers to the intensified demands to document student outcomes, calls for greater efficiency and productivity, and efforts to more closely link institutional budgets with performance as the "new accountability" movement. Growing emphases on institutional effectiveness, student outcomes, return on investment, and performance-based funding are all manifestations of the new accountability movement. The ongoing challenge for those offering remedial/developmental programs is to have useful information available to anticipate and respond to these demands for accountability.

As discussed further in Chapter Seven, developing data systems and research initiatives to respond to inquiries about the costs and benefits of these programs is important. Student information systems can be used to track student outcomes at multiple levels, including the successful completion of individual remedial/developmental courses by academic area and level; student progress in subsequent related college-level coursework; and indicators of further success, including graduation, transfer, and employment. The level of complexity in these studies grows as the researcher looks at the differences between students with a relatively minor deficiency in a single area and those with more substantial problems in multiple areas. Weakness in one academic skill area (for example, reading) may have a pronounced impact if the skill is used widely across academic coursework. Adelman (1996) notes that reading deficiencies often signal comprehensive literacy problems. Students whose academic skills on entry to college require considerable remediation can consume substantial financial aid resources to remedy basic academic skills, potentially limiting their ability to graduate. The impact of greater accountability on remedial/developmental education will not only inform policy makers of how public funds are being spent but also add to the knowledge base, encouraging instructional approaches that lead to improved student outcomes.

Technology. McCabe (1996a) notes that keeping pace with technology is an ongoing source of pressure for community college officials. There are demands to do more with fewer resources and an increase in both the number and types of competitors within a college's immediate service region. Simultaneously, increases are occurring in the numbers of underskilled students and lifelong learners attending community colleges. To provide access to these students, colleges must offer programs and services at the learner's convenience. Increasingly, extending these options involves the appropriate use of technology, which can increase costs at a time when available resources are diminishing (McCabe, 1996a, p. 5). Colleges can feel caught in a predicament where their budgets indicate an inability to afford the technology at the same time that student expectations in this area and an increasingly competitive environment suggest that colleges cannot afford to be without the technology.

Puyear (1997, p. 3) described several anticipated changes for community colleges by the year 2010 as a result of evolving technology and competition. Public, private, and commercial providers will increasingly offer educational services using a variety of nonsynchronous instructional delivery options, including "the World Wide Web, CD-ROM with an enhanced capacity, and a variety of mixed media options." Distance learning or interactive instructional television is expected to remain an essential tool for outreach to rural communities but will be largely replaced by various non-synchronous instructional delivery options (p. 3). These technologies allow students access to educational programs and services on demand. Coursework becomes increasingly structured around competencies; once those competencies are achieved, students are allowed to advance to the next level. The technology can facilitate students' abilities to acquire the requisite skills according to a self-paced schedule. Oblinger and Burnett (1995) contend that across education and training levels approximately 80 percent of instruction is done using the lecture method and suggest that multimedia technology is a viable and cost-effective alternative for some instruction.

In the future, Puyear (1997) suggests that the unit of instruction will shift toward smaller modules from the standard three-credit-hour course, that stating the specific competencies and skills associated with a course is expected to become the norm, and that flexible scheduling will be in demand to allow students to complete a given course at their own pace and move onto the next level according to their own schedule. Gianini agrees, noting that adults prefer "shorter duration, fast-paced courses with measurable results" (1997, p. 17).

The need for educational programs and services to be available on demand will have an impact on the delivery of remedial/developmental instruction. A recent study indicated that two-thirds of the community colleges in Illinois rely on full-semester-length courses for at least 90 percent of their remedial/developmental offerings (Illinois Community College Board, 1997). The traditional approach to scheduling can work well for students who take a mixture of remedial/developmental and college-level coursework simultaneously. However, such a traditional approach can be inefficient for a student needing only to refresh basic skills or to review only certain segments of a traditional course. The use of instructional technology along with a modular approach to course content can provide new avenues for students to acquire the skills they need.

Approaches to Remedial/Developmental Education

As open access institutions, community colleges have an obligation to provide remedial/developmental education for students who are underprepared for college-level work. However, political, economic, and societal pressures often cause the discharge of that obligation to be a balancing act between effectiveness and efficiency. Increasingly, federal and state agencies require greater accountability in student outcomes, while a myriad of initiatives compete for colleges' funds and the number of students who need remedial/developmental coursework remains high and requires institutions to use technology to teach effectively. College administrators are required to make difficult choices regarding the level of support available for remedial/developmental programs.

Influence of Learning Theory on Remedial/Developmental Programs. The structure of remedial/developmental programs, as well as the philosophical base on which they are built, has been heavily influenced by at least three schools of learning theory (Boylan, 1986). Remedial/developmental programs frequently use programmed instruction to varying degrees. Behaviorist theories of learning underlie the concept of programmed instruction, with the basic assumption that learners respond to external variables that can be programmed in particular ways that lead to a mastery of the subject matter. Programs founded on behavioral theory usually feature self-paced, computer-assisted instruction and, quite often, an open entry–open exit format. Programs that rely completely or substantially on a programmed instruction model are generally nonintrusive programs capable of serving large numbers of students with a minimal number of faculty and staff and are therefore relatively inexpensive to operate.

At the other end of the spectrum are programs based on developmental theories of learning. This group of theories posits that learning is a process in which individuals move from one level of knowledge to another, and that external variables can stimulate, but do not control, the learning process. The instructor plays a vital role in programs based on developmental theory by creating a supportive and encouraging environment that provides challenges at appropriate levels to stimulate learning. Obviously, such programs rely heavily on instructor involvement and, ideally, involve small classes, making them relatively expensive to offer.

Boylan (1986) points out that remedial/developmental programs are often a blend of these two theoretical models. The design of most remedial/developmental programs is based on developmental theory, but the delivery of instruction often includes instructional modes associated with behavioral theory. Such a blend can provide some cost efficiencies while still providing the support that most students in remedial/developmental education programs require.

A third model of remedial/developmental program is based on humanistic principles of learning, which assume that people are naturally inclined to learn. Programs based on humanistic theory also rely heavily on instructor involvement. However, the instructor's role is that of a manager/facilitator who creates an environment where learning will occur. The responsibility for the learning process rests primarily with the learner. Few remedial/developmental programs use this model because underprepared students are generally not ready for the responsibility of such a self-directed approach. Learning styles of developmental students tend to be more passive than those of their peers in college-level academic programs. One exception may be adult learners, who are accustomed to self-direction in other aspects of their lives, and who may accept a great deal of responsibility for their learning. Intellectual maturity appears to be a determining factor in whether an individual will benefit from a self-directed approach.

Modes of Instruction. Bers (1987) enumerates some of the many teaching modes used in remedial/developmental instruction. Self-contained classes, tutorials, computer-assisted instruction, special skills sections of existing courses, and self-paced modules are among the many formats used to deliver instruction. Each of the three theoretical approaches discussed earlier—behaviorist, developmental, and humanistic—can be used in any of the different modes of instruction.

Characteristics of Effective Remedial/Developmental Programs. Numerous studies have been conducted to determine the effectiveness of remedial/developmental programs. Most studies compare the performance of students who completed recommended remedial/developmental coursework to that of students who did not require developmental coursework. A few studies add a comparison of students who did not pursue recommended remedial/developmental coursework. In general, most studies have found that students who successfully complete recommended remedial/developmental courses perform as well as or better than college-prepared students in terms of grade point average, retention, and program completion. In fact, one important study found that students who participated in remedial/developmental programs obtained higher grades than admission criteria (such as high school rank or college-entrance examinations) would have predicted (Boylan, 1983).

A number of studies, including that of Kulik, Kulik, and Schwalb (1983), correlate effective performance with program characteristics. They found that the most effective programs involve early intervention with underprepared students, sometimes prior to college enrollment. They also found that the longer a remedial/developmental education program is in existence, the more likely it is to show positive student outcomes. Boylan (1983) found that the more comprehensive a remedial/developmental education program is, the more likely it is that students will be successful in subsequent college-level work.

A study by Roueche, Baker, and Roueche (1984) indicated a high degree of correlation between student success and the following characteristics of remedial/developmental education programs: required entry-level testing, mandatory placement in basic skills courses, a limited number of courses allowed for remediation, continuous program evaluation, and an interface between basic skills courses and subsequent college-level courses. A later study by Ross and Roe (1986) identified two additional characteristics of effective remedial/developmental education programs: a full-time director and a committed staff provided with ongoing training. Finally, a study by Tomlinson (1989) identified effective remedial/developmental education programs as offering comprehensive support services and being institutionalized within the academic mainstream. The latter characteristic is most frequently associated with support from the highest administrative levels of the institution.

Most of these characteristics are as applicable in today's environment as they were during the 1980s when they were identified by their respective authors. However, more recent approaches such as those used at Indian River Community College (Florida) and College of Lake County (Illinois) suggest that these should be expanded to include characteristics of bridge programs in which the remediation of basic skills is integrated into the curriculum and students benefit from peer support and learn through the application of basic skills to real-life situations.

Policies Common to Effective Remedial/Developmental Education Programs. As the previous section indicates, the structure of remedial/developmental education programs is an important factor in their effectiveness. Equally important to the effectiveness of the program are the institutional policies that affect the program's operation. Roueche and Roueche (1993) reviewed twelve successful community college remedial/developmental education programs as well as the current literature and concluded that the following policies had a positive effect on remedial/developmental education programs:

- Orientation should be required for entering students.
- Late registration should be abolished.
- Dual enrollment in basic skill (developmental) and college-level academic

courses should be eliminated (see comments below).

- Working students should be encouraged to reduce academic loads.
- More comprehensive financial aid opportunities should be provided for remedial/developmental students.
- Problem-solving and literacy activities should be required in all remedial/developmental courses.

Tomlinson (1989) provided additional recommendations regarding policies related to faculty and staff involved in remedial/developmental education programs:

- Involuntary placement of faculty in remedial/developmental education should be discouraged.
- Remedial/developmental education faculty should maintain contact with faculty who teach college-level courses and also should teach college-level courses when possible.
- Counselors and tutors should be available to students in remedial/developmental education throughout their program.

There is recent evidence that dual enrollment in remedial/developmental courses and college-level courses does not have a negative impact on all students. For students who are deficient in only one subject area, enrollment in college-level courses in other subject areas should not be detrimental. Boylan (1996, p. 31) recommended that, particularly for two-year institutions, the need for remediation in one area should not keep a student from pursuing regular coursework in some other area. One possible exception is the student who is deficient in reading, a vital foundational skill. What seems to be most important for students who are deficient in only one subject area is to complete the required remedial/developmental coursework early. However, for students who have multiple deficiencies, the elimination of dual enrollment makes sense. A recent study by Adelman (1996) found that students who required three or more remedial courses are at serious risk academically. Additionally, a study conducted by the College of Lake County, a public community college in Illinois, from fall 1992 through fall 1994 (described more fully in Chapter Seven of this volume), resulted in a recommendation that students who have deficiencies in two or three basic academic skill areas should be required to focus on the remediation of these deficiencies before beginning college-level coursework (Weissman, Silk, and Bulakowski, 1997). For these students, the transition to college-level courses may need to include bridge courses that emphasize both basic academic skills and subject matter.

Ideally, remedial/developmental programs should be a recognized part of institutions' academic programming supported with resources adequate to ensure that students are provided with comprehensive support services throughout their programs and possibly beyond. Appropriate technology should be incorporated into the delivery of remedial/developmental instruction. Institutions should provide committed faculty and staff with ongoing training as well as opportunities to interface with college-level faculty and curricula. Institutional policies should ensure that all students with developmental needs are identified as early as possible and are required to enroll in appropriate coursework. Institutional resources should be available as well to provide continuous evaluation of remedial/developmental programs.

Current Practice. The reality of remedial/developmental education programming is somewhat less than what the research has identified as ideal. For instance, a recent study by the National Center for Education Statistics (USDE, 1996) indicated that three-fourths of all higher education institutions surveyed required students to take remedial/developmental courses, but public two-year colleges required remediation less often than private or public four-year institutions. A recent survey of Illinois community colleges indicates that placement testing is mandatory for selected students at all public community colleges in the state (Illinois Community College Board, 1997). However, participation in remedial/developmental courses is not mandated by all colleges. The NCES study indicated that only 2 percent of all higher education institutions prohibit students from enrolling in college-level courses while enrolled in remedial/developmental courses.

The majority of higher education institutions offer remedial/developmental education through traditional academic departments. The Illinois survey indicated that 75 percent of the colleges integrate remedial/developmental education courses in academic departments (Illinois Community College Board, 1997). However, remedial/developmental courses in mathematics and writing were most likely to be offered in a separate organizational structure, and several colleges used a hybrid approach in which, for example, remedial/developmental math was part of the college's regular academic department and remedial/developmental English communications and reading were provided in a separate developmental education unit. Very few institutions provided remedial/developmental education solely through learning centers.

A consideration for the design of remedial/developmental education in the future is the increasing use of technology to customize the delivery of instruction to be convenient to the student in terms of time and location. Educators will need to identify the uses for which technology is appropriate in the delivery of remedial/developmental courses and revise or develop policies accordingly. Boylan suggested that the cost-effective delivery of remedial/developmental instruction often involves the creative use of integrated labs and computer-assisted instruction to supplement classroom instruction (1996, p. 106). Research regarding the characteristics and learning styles of students, as well as documented patterns of academic performance for various groups of students, may be helpful. For example, students, particularly adults, with identified skill deficiencies in only one subject area may be very successful in computer-assisted courses or in self-paced courses delivered by television or the Internet. On the other hand, students with multiple deficiencies may need to attend classes where they interact with an instructor and are offered extensive guidance and feedback. Clearly, students exhibit a range of needs in the area of remedial/developmental instruction for which there is no one-size-fits-all solution, including the use of technology.

Conclusion

The purpose of this chapter has been to examine remedial/developmental education within the current community college environment and explore various approaches for delivery of remedial/developmental programs. There is little doubt that substantial numbers of students entering community colleges and other institutions of higher education are not adequately prepared to undertake college-level coursework. Some of the major policy questions surrounding this situation are at the center of debate within the current political, social, and educational environment. *Why should additional tax dollars be spent teaching students skills they are expected to acquire in high school? Is it more cost-effective to restrict remedial/developmental education delivery to community colleges? Should the number of remedial/developmental courses supported by tax dollars be restricted?*

Although these questions are legitimate, the reality of the situation is that providing educational access and addressing the needs of students must be the driving force behind policy decisions. As long as there are indications that students have the potential to be successful in collegiate-level coursework if deficiencies are remedied, community colleges have the responsibility to respond to these students' needs. The question then becomes, how can the college best assist students in overcoming these deficiencies with the current environment demanding more accountability and technological facility from the institution?

Colleges must provide an environment that supports student learning while at the same time being accountable to the public and the student for the outcomes of their efforts. Students are asking for educational opportunities that are flexible and that will permit them to accomplish their goals as quickly as possible. The use of technology along with flexible scheduling can assist in providing these opportunities. Of all higher education institutions, community colleges are the most likely to offer remedial/developmental education courses in the evening, on weekends, and during the summer (USDE, 1996).

Research has identified program characteristics and institutional policies that are associated with effective remedial/developmental education programming. The challenge to individual institutions is to blend the ideal with reality in a way that maximizes student success. The preceding discussion has explored possible ways to accomplish this goal. Recognizing the needs of students and developing policies that ensure appropriate levels of intervention for groups of students with different needs is the key to maximizing the effectiveness and efficiency of remedial/developmental programs.

References

Adelman, C. "The Truth About Remedial Work: It's More Complex Than Windy Rhetoric and Simple Solutions Suggest." *The Chronicle of Higher Education,* Oct. 4, 1996, p. A56.

Ansley, A. "They Came to College? A Remedial/Developmental Profile of First-Time Freshmen in SREB States." *Issues in Higher Education,* 1991, 25. (ED 333 783)

Bers, T. *Evaluating Remedial Education Programs.* AIR Professional File. Tallahassee: Florida State University, 1987.

Boylan, H. R. *Is Developmental Education Working?: An Analysis of the Research.* Research report no. 2. Chicago: National Association of Developmental Education, 1983.

Boylan, H. R. "Theoretical Foundations of Developmental Education." *Research in Developmental Education,* 1986, 3.

Boylan, H. R. *An Evaluation of the Texas Academic Skills Program (TASP).* Boone, North Carolina: National Center for Developmental Education at Appalachian State University, 1996.

Drucker, P. "The Age of Social Transformation." *The Atlantic Monthly,* Nov. 1994, pp. 53–80.

Ewell, P. T. *Assessment and the New Accountability: A Challenge for Higher Education Leadership.* Denver: Education Commission of the States, 1990.

Finn, C. E., Jr. "The Conflicting Values of Consumers and Producers." *Educational Record,* 1997, 78 (1), 11–16.

Gianini, P. C., Jr. "Economic Development: A Postmodern Dilemma." *Community College Journal,* 1997, 67 (6), 14–18.

Illinois Community College Board. *Remedial/Developmental Education in the Illinois Community College System: Scope, Cost, Structure, Outcomes, and Policies.* Springfield: Illinois Community College Board, 1997.

Kulik, C. C., Kulik, J. A., and Schwalb, B. J. "College Programs for High-Risk and Disadvantaged Students: A Meta-Analysis of Findings." *Review of Educational Research,* fall 1983, pp. 397–414.

Maryland Higher Education Commission. *A Study of Remedial Education at Maryland Public Campuses.* Annapolis: Maryland Higher Education Commission, 1996.

McCabe, R. "Communications Technology and Distance Learning Will Systematically Change Community Colleges." *Community College Week,* Mar. 11, 1996a, p. 5.

McCabe, R. "Remedial Programs Essential to Quality Community College Programs." *Community College Week,* Feb. 12, 1996b, pp. 4–13.

Oblinger, D., and Burnett, D. "Technology as the Catalyst: Creating a Student-Centered Environment." Presentation at the Association of Community College Trustees Convention, Seattle, Washington, Sep. 1995.

Puyear, D. E. "Community Colleges in 2010." *Community College Times,* Feb. 25, 1997, pp. 3, 6.

"Remedial Remedies." *Community College Week,* Jan. 13, 1997, p. 11.

Reyes, N. "Texas Report Questions Remedial Programs' Success." *Community College Week,* Nov.18, 1996, pp. 2, 11.

Ross, F. P., and Roe, B. D. "The Case for Basic Skills Programs in Higher Education." *Fastback 238.* Bloomington, Indiana: Phi Delta Kappa Educational Foundation, 1986.

Roueche, J. E., Baker, G. A., III, and Roueche, S. D. *College Responses to Low-Achieving Students.* New York: Harcourt, Brace & Jovanovich, 1984.

Roueche, J. E., and Roueche, S. *Between a Rock and a Hard Place: The At-Risk Student in the Open-Door College.* Washington, D.C.: The Community College Press, 1993.

Ruppert, S. S. (ed.). *Charting Higher Education Accountability: A Sourcebook on State-Level Performance Indicators.* Denver: Education Commission of the States, 1994.

Schoenecker, C., Bollman, L., and Evens, J. "Developmental Education Outcomes at Minnesota Community Colleges." Presentation at the Annual Forum of the Association for Institutional Research, New Orleans, May 1996.

Steinberg, B. "Remediation Problems Growing in Maryland." *Community College Week*, Nov. 18, 1996, p.10.

Tomlinson, L. M. *Postsecondary Developmental Programs: A Traditional Agenda with New Imperatives.* Report 3. Washington, D.C.: School of Education and Human Development, The George Washington University, 1989.

U.S. Department of Education, National Center for Education Statistics. *Remedial Education at Higher Education Institutions in Fall 1995,* NCES 97–584, by L. Lewis and E. Farris. Washington, D.C.: U.S. Government Printing Office, 1996.

Weissman, J., Silk, E., and Bulakowski, C. "Assessing Developmental Education Policies." *Research in Higher Education,* 1997, *38* (2), 187–200.

VIRGINIA K. MCMILLAN *is deputy executive director of the Illinois Community College Board.*

SCOTT J. PARKE *is director for policy studies at the Illinois Community College Board.*

CAROL A. LANNING *is director for program planning and accountability at the Illinois Community College Board.*

In the presence of internal and external controversy, the decision to move from a system of open enrollment to a system of mandatory placement is difficult; once the decision is made, implementation presents its own difficulties.

Mandatory Assessment and Placement: The View from an English Department

Dorothy M. Berger

In the fall 1997 semester, the San Diego Community College District began to implement a system of mandatory placement in all English classes at its three colleges. This means that students who have not met a prerequisite are blocked from enrolling in classes. (A prerequisite may be met either by satisfactorily completing a lower-level course or by achieving a specified skill level, which is computed by formula from assessment test scores and various details of student academic history.) The district is also enforcing prerequisites in about seventy other courses, primarily in the sciences and languages, that would lose transferability if the prerequisites are not enforced. Subsequent semesters will see increasing numbers of courses in which students cannot register without having met the prerequisite, including many courses across the curriculum that either require or advise students to have reached a specified level in English. This change marks the end of a period in which prerequisites appeared in the catalogs but were treated as advisory only and were not enforced.

Reactions to this change in policy range from relief to dismay to trepidation, an indication that although implementation will occur, broad consensus does not yet exist. English faculty in particular expect a decline in the number of students who disappear before the end of a semester and an increase in the quality of students' work. Many administrators have deep and serious concerns about the legal, ethical, and financial ramifications of enforcement, including a decline in enrollment. These differing views are emblematic of a national discussion known variously as the "access versus success" or "access versus standards" argument, in which a central question is whether students benefit most from being free to enroll as they wish or from having the institution take a prescriptive role in their progress through the curriculum. When colleges choose a prescriptive role, the issue is how to ensure that this intervention does not block students from access or create discouraging hurdles after enrollment.

The San Diego Community College District's sometimes tortuous five-year path back to mandatory placement reflects some aspects of the access versus standards argument that may be typical only of California or only of the San Diego Community College District. The philosophical and implementational aspects of the access versus standards argument are not unique, however, nor is the interplay of the internal and external factors that modulate the discussion; thus an examination of one system's response to that nationwide argument may illustrate its complexities and ironies in a way that is useful to individuals and systems on all sides of the issue.

The Setting and Some Relevant History

The San Diego Community College District comprises three colleges—City College, Mesa College, and Miramar College—six Continuing Education Centers (which do not figure in this account), and a central administrative office under the direction of a chancellor. The district is governed by a locally elected Board of Trustees, and each college has its own president and its own academic senate. The colleges enroll about 43,500 students, and there are about 2400 full- and part-time faculty. Ethnically, the district is relatively similar to California community colleges in general: 45.8 percent of the student population is white, 15.4 percent is Latino, 11.6 percent is African American, 12.1 percent is Asian/Pacific Islander, 6.4 percent is Filipino, and 1.5 percent is American Indian. A central issue is, of course, how an organization of this size, heterogeneity, and structure comes to consensus on any issue, much less such a sensitive one as mandatory assessment and placement.

The Previous, Non-Mandatory Placement System. The last ten or so years have seen a largely unintended decline in the degree to which course and skill-level prerequisites have been enforced, ending in an open system with students completely free to choose what level of courses in which to enroll. (One exception has been some vocational programs that have continued to be strictly monitored.) The initial stage of the change was not the result of a philosophical shift but rather a function of changes in the registration system. In the days of in-person registration, when a counselor's signature was required each semester, counselors exerted a large measure of control if they wished to. They could, after discussion with a student, decide whether to enforce or waive a prerequisite. Shifting students after the beginning of a semester was common in English classes if faculty felt that students had enrolled at an inappropriate level. The advent of mail-in registration in 1987 relaxed this already somewhat porous system, as did word that a suit (to be discussed more fully in a later section) had been filed against the California community college system. The account that circulated among the faculty was that a charge had been filed claiming that a prerequisite for a freshman composition course was discriminatory, but the details of the suit were not clearly or widely understood.

Instructions to faculty changed so that in the early days of a semester they could only recommend that a student enroll in a different course—they could not insist. The advent of an electronic telephone registration system in 1994 and the clear but somewhat delayed understanding that the district was no longer in compliance with changed regulations about prerequisites meant, finally, that students could enroll as they wished. The telephone registration system advised students when they had not met a prerequisite, but it did not block enrollment.

The Reaction of English Faculty.   Resignation, frustration, and despair are not traditional subjects of research or policy writing in higher education. Yet these terms characterize the ongoing reactions of English faculty during the years in which more and more students enrolled in courses for which they were unprepared. The English faculty were generally aware of the access versus standards discussion going on nationally, but like many colleagues, their primary focus was and is the classroom. Few saw the immediate situation as part of a larger phenomenon, believing, rather, that local administrators were uninterested in or unaware of the daily challenges to academic standards. Faculty also felt that instituting mandatory placement in their classes would be relatively simple to organize. At the beginning of any semester, it often appeared that only a small handful of students in a class of thirty-two were likely to pass the course. Even if that impression were exaggerated, under those circumstances it was difficult to plan lectures and assignments knowing that they would be above (or below) the capacity of many in the class. The colleges have made tutoring and support services increasingly available over the years, but when a student enrolls significantly above his or her level of readiness, no amount of tutoring and no amount of dedication by the faculty can enable that student to master simultaneously the material in the current course and that of two or more prerequisite courses. Faculty grumbled that those teaching at lower levels were passing students who were unprepared for the next course in the sequence—even though all members of the department were teaching at more than one level and were thus both subject and object of the complaint. Instructors in the two levels of remedial reading and writing courses found their classes largely populated by students who should have been in English as a second language (ESL) classes but who, in their eagerness to progress, preferred not to take them. ESL instructors found that students often skipped the two lowest levels of ESL and enrolled simultaneously in two higher-level sequential courses. Other students would fail a course at one level but enroll nevertheless in the next highest level, fail that, and move on again.

Faculty were often in a quandary regarding what final grade to give a student who would have been appropriately enrolled in a lower level but who had made significant progress over the course of a semester. If the student had still not achieved the goals of the course he or she was enrolled in, a failing grade penalized hard work and accomplishment, but a passing grade inaccurately signaled the student's level of competence. Many faculty felt that their ability to carry out their professional responsibilities had been compromised. In the face of what appeared to be severely confounded placement, faculty began to lose their own sense of standards at each level of the curriculum. Clear evidence about the loss of consensus on exit standards manifested itself in such things as department workshops in which different faculty members would grade the same sample student essay variously from a D to a B. The situation was particularly troubling to the large numbers of part-time faculty, who feared that if they failed large numbers of students or had unusually high attrition rates, their jobs would be in jeopardy.

The phrase "dumbing down" has entered our common vocabulary, but it does not capture the anguish (sometimes resigned cynicism) of a faculty that feels itself forced to participate in a lowering of standards, all the while decrying the phenomenon.

Still, with the exception of an occasional dramatic outburst in college or district meetings, discussion of the apparent erosion of standards was largely limited to department meetings, hallway conversations, and faculty dining rooms, and the response was often that faculty have always complained about their students or that the evidence was merely anecdotal. Data were only recently produced that confirmed the faculty's assertion that large numbers of students ignored prerequisites.

The Impetus to Mandate Placement. Despite consistent pressure from the faculty to resume enforcement of prerequisites, the real impetus to do so came from a chain of legal and legislative events, enacted in the statewide arena of the same access versus standards argument that was occurring locally in the San Diego Community College District. When the California legislature passed the Seymour-Campbell Matriculation Act of 1986, it was seen as an assertion of the advocates of "standards" in its requirements for such things as assessment, educational plans filed by students, orientation, and counseling—all designed to move more community college students more expeditiously toward their educational goals. A response from the proponents of "access" followed in 1988, when MALDEF, The Mexican American Legal Defense and Educational Fund, filed suit against the chancellor of the California Community Colleges, the statewide Board of Governors, and others, claiming that they were using assessment tests and other aspects of matriculation in a discriminatory fashion to block Hispanic students from access to college-level courses. The suit did not go to trial, but the settlement in 1991 had far-reaching effects in substantial revisions to the state matriculation regulations (Cage, 1991). The changes were so complex that the State Chancellor's Office prepared a model policy that local community college districts could adopt or adapt in confidence of acting within the new regulations. For colleges choosing to enforce prerequisites, the major requirements were the following (Matriculation Regulations Review Task Force, 1993):

- The governing board must adopt a policy on the matter, and students must be widely advised of its provisions.
- Only placement tests approved by the State Chancellor's Office may be used, and the tests need to be locally validated.

- Placement may not be based on a single measure such as a score on a test but must be made according to multiple measures, which may not correlate highly with one another.
- Prerequisites may be set only following a course-by-course scrutiny of outlines, textbooks, examinations, syllabi, and the like, ending in a clear listing of entry and exit skills for each course.
- Communication or mathematics prerequisites for courses outside English and mathematics departments may not be adopted in a blanket provision across the curriculum and, when imposed, must be based on research that shows their applicability to student success in each specific course.
- Students must be permitted to challenge prerequisites.
- Determination of a student's having met or not met a prerequisite must be made prior to enrollment in a course.
- Prerequisites must be reviewed regularly, at least once each six years.
- When precollegiate courses serve as prerequisites, they must be offered in reasonable proportion to the number of students who need them.
- There must be a formal agreement by the faculty to teach according to approved course outlines, particularly in those aspects of a course most directly related to the prerequisite.

The intent of these provisions is clear: in an attempt to balance access and academic standards, the regulations hold that prerequisites, as potential barriers to access, should not be capriciously or carelessly set or set permanently without review. If students are required to have certain skills or bodies of knowledge before they may take a particular class, that class should, in fact, operate in such a manner that those skills or knowledge are actually needed for success. Yet many in the district felt (and may still feel) that these provisions were unnecessarily burdensome and complex, designed more to discourage implementation of prerequisites than to ensure equity. For example, approximately 1700 course outlines in ninety-eight programs needed to be individually scrutinized, and that process needed to be documented and made available for inspection. An additional requirement was that the results for each course had to be approved, prior to catalog printing deadlines, in separate actions by three separate curriculum committees. This presented a daunting organizational challenge in a district this size. Many faculty felt the process to be an unwarranted intrusion into professional judgment. The ability to read and write at the college level before taking, say, a history or philosophy course seemed so self-evident that the requirement to do research to demonstrate the connection was shocking. Nevertheless, the process was begun.

The Process

Over a period of several years, various ad hoc committees were formed, dissolved, and reconstituted, the Board of Trustees adopted a policy on prerequisites, staff from the Research and Planning Office worked with English and math department chairs to validate the placement tests and choose multiple measures, a committee wrote a challenge procedure, and a scrutiny procedure was established that held each academic dean responsible for calling together faculty in like disciplines from each of the three colleges to decide whether to keep, alter, or eliminate prerequisites and to write specific exit skills for each course. There were arguments about the meaning of research reports. For example, if a correlation study indicated no relationship between reading or writing ability and success in, say, a political science class, did that mean that English skills were irrelevant or that standards had been seriously compromised? Curriculum committees went into overtime operation, surrounded by mountains of paper since the scrutiny packet for each course was at least ten pages long. At one point, in 1996, because the English and mathematics departments had completed the process first and were eager, agreement was reached that prerequisites for those two departments would be enforced on a pilot basis the next fall. At the last minute, however, implementation was postponed for a year as the implications of enforcement became clearer and district and college leadership voiced concern that preparation was insufficient.

During that year, it became apparent that although an enormous amount of time and energy had already been expended on the practical preparations for mandated placement, the district had had insufficiently broad discussions on the philosophical aspects of the matter and commitment to implementation was uncertain. It is true that the trustees had adopted a policy, and there had been periodic reports on progress, but it may be that the intense activity and the periodic nature of the reporting had somehow masked the failure to ascertain whether consensus existed. It may also be that as the practical consequences of mandating placement became apparent, anxiety about how far-reaching those consequences would be triggered new questioning about the philosophical basis of the entire undertaking.

Additional External Factors. Also during that year, a second major external factor became apparent. In 1988 the California legislature approved regulations designed to significantly increase the role of academic senates in the community colleges. The concept of shared governance requires that boards of trustees consult collegially with the academic senates on a broad spectrum of issues outside the scope of collective bargaining. This concept has had a troubled history in California (Trombley, 1997). However, the San Diego Community College District has made serious efforts to implement the provisions of shared governance, although a full understanding has not come quickly, either to the faculty or the administration. Nevertheless, during the past year new ways of interaction between the faculty senates and district administration were emerging. Though there has not been a sharp, districtwide faculty-administration split on the issue of enforcing prerequisites, in discussions between the district administrators and the senate presidents, the voice of the faculty was strengthened and supported by the existence of district policy that includes "standards or policies regarding student preparation and success" among the topics on which the "Board shall . . . rely primarily upon the advice and judgment of the Senates" (San Diego Community College District, 1992, pp. 1–2).

A third external factor has been the role of the four-year colleges and universities to which community college students transfer. During the years when prerequisites were not being enforced, faculty had frequently voiced their fear that courses would lose transferability, but from the perspective of the faculty, the receiving transfer institutions were largely—and curiously—silent. It appeared that so long as prerequisites remained in the catalogs, irrespective of whether they were being enforced, transferability would remain. Various contradictory and ambiguous signals arrived from time to time, and the universities seemed indecisive. Very late in the final year of planning and discussion, when the issue of which, if any, prerequisites would be enforced, a dramatic, unequivocal communication from the University of California settled the matter: Transfer and articulation agreements that included prerequisites would be invalidated if the community colleges did not enforce them (L. Randolph, office communication, Feb. 27, 1997). A major, almost instantaneous shift occurred in the district's stance. Although many still objected to or feared rigorous enforcement, loss of transfer was obviously unthinkable and accommodation to a new reality had to be accepted.

Thus the situation had come full circle: An external legal challenge to enforced prerequisites had resulted first in a cessation of enforcement, then in major introspection by the faculty and staff of the district; and a tentative, reluctant, sometimes wavering movement back toward strictly enforced prerequisites—long desired by many in the ranks of the faculty—became a necessity in order to maintain transferability. The initial claim of unlawful discrimination by virtue of limitations on access (the MALDEF suit) has resulted, ironically, in much tighter (albeit better thought-out) control of students' progress through the curriculum.

The Practical Implications of Enforcing Prerequisites. Reaching the decision to enforce prerequisites was such a time- and energy-consuming process that both district and college personnel were somewhat slow to realize the extent of the practical and financial arrangements that would be necessary as a result, and a system already operating under high pressure moved into a higher level of anxiety. One such practical implication was the realization that since about 15 percent of the students enter as transfers from other institutions, they need to submit their transcripts prior to enrollment if they have met various prerequisites elsewhere. Current staffing in the Evaluations Offices is, however, not large enough to prevent massive bottlenecks. Staff in the Testing Offices will also have to be increased to handle dramatic increases in placement testing. The challenge procedure refers all challenges to the departments, but the bulk of challenges will occur during summer and winter breaks when faculty are not on duty. Significant reallocation of funds will be needed.

A very serious implication of enforcement of prerequisites will be the shift in the balance of sections of transfer and remedial courses in the English department and the probable need for an increased number of sections. Everyone knew that the balance would shift, but the magnitude of the shift (though not completely clear at the time of this writing) is startling. Based on test results, projections are that the number of sections of remedial reading and writing could increase by a factor of three. Because students have chosen, in increasing numbers over the years, to bypass these lowest levels of classes, few among the current faculty have sufficient experience and training in the characteristics of developmental students and the specific techniques of teaching them. Retraining or at least resensitization to issues of remediation has become a necessity because these students will no longer be dispersed throughout other courses. And, of course, the issue of increasing English offerings has become an internal political issue, other departments fearing that the increase will come at their expense. There is talk—only partly in jest—of the growing imperialism of the English departments. But an overriding concern is the requirement in state regulations that when pre-transfer courses are designated as prerequisites, they must be readily available, the issue again being not to limit access. Predicting how to schedule for the first semester with enforced prerequisites is proving to be extremely difficult. Will new students' reaction be to delay taking English, to enroll in higher numbers, or to flock to colleges in nearby districts where prerequisites are not being enforced? And what plans can be made for making possibly large changes at the opening of the semester if the best predictions turn out to be seriously incorrect? At the time of this writing, all of these issues are still being resolved.

Potential Outcomes

It is, of course, too early to know if this process will have the intended outcome: increased rates of student success without reduced access to the colleges. And it is clear that many aspects of the process were less than satisfactory. It is difficult, however, to move quickly in a straight line through a field so charged with uncertainties and conflicts. Great care needs to be taken when the lives of so many students are to be affected. But some important benefits are already clear. Instructional research has increased, as has the faculty's ability to interpret it. Interaction among colleagues in the district's three colleges and administrative headquarters has increased, in some instances dramatically. There is also increased interaction with the staffs of nearby and not so nearby transfer institutions and community colleges. Most important is the experience of broad, honest wrestling with ideas lying at the heart of what we do, ideas that are often subordinated to the dailiness of teaching and administration. The adherents of "access" and the adherents of "standards" now look and feel less like armed camps and more like people with differences that they know can be resolved.

References

Cage, M. C. "California Community Colleges System Agrees to Change Role of Testing." *Chronicle of Higher Education,* June 12, 1991, p. A21.

Matriculation Regulations Review Task Force. "The Model District Policy." Sacramento: The Community College Chancellor's Office, 1993.

San Diego Community College District. "Shared Governance." Policy No. 0003, July 9, 1992.

Trombley, W. " 'Shared Governance': An Elusive Goal." *Crosstalk,* 1997, 5 (1), 7–14.

DOROTHY M. BERGER *is chair of the English Department at San Diego Mesa College.*

This chapter describes an interventionist system implemented by a large suburban community college to respond to underprepared students. Rather than ignoring the problems of underprepared students and relegating them to second-class status, the college worked at connecting and supporting all students equally to demonstrate that intrusive and interventionist policies need not be punitive.

Structured Versus Laissez-Faire Open Access: Implementation of a Proactive Strategy

Richard Fonte

Many strategies have been attempted at community colleges to assist students to achieve their educational objectives. However, with an increasing number of entering community college students underprepared for college-level academic work, developmental education has become a critical element of most approaches. Community colleges have developed student success systems for an increasingly at-risk student body that combine student service retention programs with developmental education.

A major variation among colleges is the degree to which efforts are mandatory and universally applied. Some differences may stem from resource availability, but more frequently they derive from conflicting philosophical outlooks. Any review of the issues that impact on policy for developmental education must first begin, therefore, with a discussion of the open access enrollment principle intrinsic to the mission of community colleges.

The Open Access Debate

Community colleges that maintain that an "open door" requires unlimited access to all courses, and even a right to fail, oppose mandatory student success strategies (Richardson, 1988, p. 28; Roueche and Roueche, 1994, p. 6). The viewpoint, which rejects restrictions limiting course-taking access, might well be called *laissez-faire open access*. Virtually all developmental education strategies under this orientation are voluntary and nondirective. Implementation of programs aimed at enhancing student academic achievement in college, including developmental education, are dependent on the student's accepting advice from an empathetic counselor or professional.

The contrasting perspective, which relies on a caring but intrusive system of facilitating student achievement (Lopez, Yanez, Clayton, and Thompson, 1988), may be designated "structured open access." Strategies under this view utilize mandatory policies and proactive, interventionist practices for developmental education and other student services. Student academic achievement and retention in college are thought to be enhanced through consistent and universal application of concepts that have demonstrated clear success at many other colleges. Advocates argue that this position is the more effective approach to maximizing student educational goal accomplishment (Roueche and Roueche, 1993, 1994).

Student success programs can be classified by both their characteristics and their purposes. A four-category typology suggested by P. Beatty-Guenter (1994) has divided efforts that connect, support, sort, or transform students. A review of the tactics under each of these classifications reveals that many can be applied either under a structured or laissez-faire open access orientation.

Developmental education, obviously, falls under the *transforming* category, and is usually delivered in an environment that includes other strategies for helping students succeed in college. *Connecting* retention activities, such as organized student activities that help students get to know others on campus, are clearly voluntary, although advising programs and new student orientation programs can be either required or optional. Whereas most of the *supporting* retention strategies, such as child care, are nonintrusive, financial aid can involve directive academic performance standards for continued student eligibility.

The strategies of sorting by an academic standard and transformation of academic ability stimulate a great deal of ideological discussion. Sorting tactics, including assessing students at entry, using prerequisites, and monitoring academic progress, can be administered in an environment that leads to either voluntary recommendations to students or compulsory requirements. Likewise, transforming approaches, including developmental education and tutoring, can be either voluntary or obligatory programs.

Mandatory sorting and transforming activities lead to differential treatment of designated students based on academic criteria. These approaches, in particular, raise the question of student tracking and the class replication critique advanced by Karabel (1972) and others. Are students who score lower on entry assessment tracked into developmental education and then channeled into occupational rather than baccalaureate programs? Is it the case that "counselors and administrators enroll students in occupational courses that do not require basic skills proficiency" (Kingan and Alfred, 1993, p. 7)? Of course, such "cooling out" advising could be undertaken within a voluntary or permissive context, but it becomes a very serious issue in a mandatory and structured environment.

The Structured Open Access Model

The *structured open access* philosophy answers the class replication critics by applying its principles to all programs, both transfer baccalaureate and career occupational. Advocates of access with standards and structure, such as Richardson (1988), Eaton (1988), and Cohen and Brawer (1987), maintain that the defining characteristic of college-level study at any community college demands that the academic standard of college-level work be applied to both transfer and career students.

Research has demonstrated that the most effective student success plans involve a blend of strategies (Beatty-Guenter, 1994). The philosophy of adding structure while preserving access, labeled here *structured open access,* suggests the systematic use of academic standards linked with additional approaches to assist students to reach their educational objectives. Supporters maintain that designs combining mandatory sorting by academic criteria with directive, interventionist tactics of transforming, supporting, or connecting students actually increase rather than limit student achievement.

The structured open access perspective has been applied at many community colleges in varying degrees. In fact, the pure laissez-faire open access institution may now be virtually nonexistent. Therefore, most community colleges can probably be placed on a continuum between these two approaches in their student success practices. Colleges that have few exemptions from a universal policy for all students would tend toward the structured open access model, and schools with many exceptions or only limited application of mandatory prescriptions would be more laissez-faire.

Implementation of the Structured Open Access Model

A college wishing to operate under structured open access principles must adopt a set of intrusive and proactive policies. South Suburban College, a community college in Illinois with a large number of underprepared students along with a significant minority student population, adopted this model in the early 1990s following a very thorough review of the literature of retention and student success strategies. In fact, each of the fourteen campus policies outlined below were adapted from approaches utilized at other colleges. They represent a very comprehensive set of strategies that any other college seeking to adopt a structured open access philosophy may wish to review.

South Suburban College utilized mandatory strategies involving sorting and transforming students and also mandatory connecting and supporting approaches. The college depended on an empowered counseling staff to make decisions under a system of standards. Although departures from the policies were possible with counselor approval, the collegewide adoption of an intrusive philosophy made such exceptions to mandatory interventions well deliberated and unusual.

Sorting and Transforming Policies. The placement testing and developmental education policies at the college were designed to be mandatory, prescriptive, and comprehensive. Previous procedures had had a limited impact on only a small segment of the total student enrollment. Under the comprehensive design, up-front assessment could not be avoided by certificate and degree seekers, whether full- or part-time. The strategy was implemented through an effective computer system that supported mandatory course sequencing. The key principle was that developmental coursework, especially reading and writing, should occur as soon as the student begins college coursework. Moreover, the policy established the primary place of reading within the developmental education sequence.

Policy 1: Mandatory placement testing is required for all degree-seeking students. The college required the ACT ASSET placement test of *all* certificate- or degree-seeking students prior to registration in any course at the college. Even the self-identified group of students who indicated they were only taking a few courses were required to take the placement test if they attempted to register for a seventh hour. In effect, such students were presumed to have moved toward a definitive educational objective and were beyond an experimenting stage. Moreover, because of the commitment to mandatory placement testing prior to registration, Touch-tone telephone registration was restricted to those not requiring a placement test or other counselor intervention.

The registration application (and also the phone registration script) used for each registration required students to indicate their degree or certificate intentions or "course-taking only" status. This datum directed the computer to block enrollment for any student who had not taken the placement test.

The strategy of mandatory and universal test taking was aimed at having students discover early their own barriers to successful achievement of educational goals. The policy is based on the principle that students will be more successful in college if they address remediation on entry to the college. Many other designs have failed to recognize that some students without declared degree intentions have nonetheless devised an informal plan by the time they take their third course. If the college does not have automatic intervention procedures, such students could fall well behind before a test-taking policy could identify an educational problem.

Policy 2: A supplemental writing sample test is required for students who score within specific "decision zones" on the entrance writing test. A writing sample evaluated by English department faculty supplemented the ASSET English assessment for students whose scores fell within the range between developmental English and college-level English. A writing sample was also employed for those individuals who scored at the lowest developmental level of reading but who, somewhat surprisingly, had placed into college English. The writing sample supplement strengthened the overall initial assessment. The use of a second evaluation for borderline students increased reliability without excessively increasing costs and numbers assessed. This addition protected the college against the criticism of using a single standard when mandatory policies with high consequences were being applied.

Policy 3: High school transcripts are required of all degree-seeking students. Proper placement, especially in math and English, was enhanced with critical information provided through high school transcripts. The transcript request became part of the total application and admissions process. Walk-in registration enrollees were also asked to sign a transcript request form as part of the registration process. All available transcripts were used during the mandatory orientation or course-planning session following placement testing. Transcript analysis of all entering degree-seeking students was also necessary to determine whether they were to be admitted under full or provisional admissions status under new Illinois college admissions standards. Provisionally admitted students were informed of their course deficiencies and were advised of appropriate class selections needed to eliminate provisional status. The use of transcripts represented an appraisal beyond standardized testing that strengthened the case for mandatory decision making by providing supplemental information for borderline situations. This information provided counselors with data to make well-deliberated decisions and a basis for exceptions to the general policy.

Policy 4: Developmental courses are mandatory beginning with the student's first semester. A developmental sequence was established that required a student to take at least one developmental course each semester until the student completed any required non-college-level developmental coursework. The student was required to take reading before any other developmental coursework and writing before math. Obviously, no college-level math or English course could be taken until a student had completed developmental work in these areas. The registration system would not allow an enrollment transaction to be completed unless a developmental course was part of the enrollment transaction. Although counselors were empowered to make exceptions, especially for math in programs not heavily dependent on math competency, the overall thrust was to move students through developmental coursework early in their college career.

Policy 5: Early completion of the developmental reading sequence is mandated and considered essential for future college success. If a student placed into developmental reading in either of two groupings—level 1, or sixth- and seventh-grade reading levels, and level 2, or eighth- and ninth-grade reading levels—the student had to take developmental reading during that first semester. Students who tested below the sixth-grade reading level (the federal "ability to benefit" standard) were restricted to taking an intensive reading course offered through the college's noncredit adult education division.

Reading classes offered at level 2 had a discipline emphasis (for example, health and science readings). More difficult to develop and offer, specialized level 2 reading courses provided a stronger link to college-level coursework than generic reading courses. Moreover, because under the policy the developmental student had to complete the developmental reading sequence, the higher-level reading courses needed to demonstrate linkage to college coursework.

This policy endorsed the principle that an adequate reading level is *the* critical element in classroom success. Because most college textbooks are written at a minimum tenth-grade reading level, students reading below that level experience difficulty comprehending critical material in any college course. In a proactive environment, mandatory developmental reading courses have become the fundamental building blocks of developmental programs.

Policy 6: Developmental students with significant pre-collegiate coursework requirements are considered at-risk students and have both course and credit load restrictions. Any student who tested both at the developmental reading and developmental English level was limited to taking ten credit hours, which had to include developmental reading. Associate in arts or associate in science degree transfer students were also required to take a one-credit college success course. Any student placing in developmental reading at the first level (less than eighth-grade reading) was further restricted in course selection to a short list of non-reading-intensive classes and limited to ten credit hours. For those students identified at the very lowest levels of reading (below the sixth grade), dual enrollment in college credit and developmental classes was blocked by the computer registration system. Full concurrent registration in credit classes was permitted only for those at the highest level of developmental reading. The college counselors were responsible for implementing this policy and working closely with students who were most at risk.

This clear example of a proactive policy thoroughly rejected the right to fail principle, which would have allowed at-risk, low-reading-level students to take heavy course loads or reading-intensive coursework.

Connecting and Supporting Policies. The early-warning and academic progress information systems communicated with students both early and frequently throughout their academic careers. College services were activated to assist those experiencing academic difficulty as early as practical in their careers. The objective was to provide a comprehensive and mandatory set of connecting and supportive retention and academic support programs for at-risk students. The policies and programs aimed at tracking student academic progress were *front-loaded* (that is, begun early in a student's college career) and have been especially significant for students enrolled in developmental coursework. The front-loading principle was extended to recognize that students need feedback on academic progress during a semester as well as after a semester. An additional connecting concept focused on student intent and the mandatory creation of a formal educational plan for all students at the beginning of their college careers, including those requiring developmental education.

Policy 7: The academic alert and intervention system must occur at the start of every student's academic career to equalize services to both full- and part-time students. The college's policy of academic warning, the first level of the academic alert and intervention system, was changed so that it began at the seventh credit hour. The policy recognized that part-time students, carrying substantial loads, had in the past not received sufficient institutional attention. This included many students who were enrolled in developmental classes. Under past policies, which initiated efforts only after twelve credit hours, part-time students might not receive college retention services until their third or fourth semester. The seventh-hour policy has tended to equalize services to part-timers, who in the past may have been more likely to drop out prior to receiving intervention services. Whereas full-timers still received services at the same time as under previous policies, the part-timer carrying a load of three courses was now intercepted after the first semester. Because a part-timer frequently has many other outside responsibilities, such as a full-time job, the earlier intervention strategy and mandatory counseling and advising services could be critical to continued retention for such students.

This policy became pivotal as the college moved toward front-loaded policies on developmental education. The twelfth-hour trigger was a historical vestige that assumed that students were predominately full-time. The seventh-hour trigger is realistic for community college students who often come underprepared for college-level work and need to enroll early in developmental coursework.

Policy 8: Students on academic warning or probation status are required to develop an action plan to improve their academic standing. Students placed on either academic warning or academic probation were sent letters explaining their status and requirements for registering for an additional semester. The students were required to see a counselor prior to further registration and to develop a co-signed (student and counselor) action plan aimed at returning the student to good academic standing. Such students could not use Touchtone registration because of the required counselor intervention. Counselors were given the authority to require specific transforming actions as a condition of continued registration, including tutoring, work study workshops, follow-up counseling sessions, and specific developmental courses. The action plan requirements were recorded in the computer system.

This policy, along with policy 6, depended on an empowered counseling staff. Rather than limiting counselors, structured access policies required intervention by counselors, enhanced their professionalism, and targeted student success efforts. Counselors have found involvement rewarding because of the clearer systems of tracking at-risk students and the feedback of their prescriptive recommendations.

Policy 9: Course-load credit hour limits are "presumptive recommendations" within each action plan. Load limits were placed on students who were on academic warning or academic probation. The action plan prescriptions were considered maximums unless waived by a counselor. The load limits varied, based on the previous semester's GPA and the student's academic standing. A student in serious academic difficulty, however, could have his or her credit load limited to as few as four credits, or one course, as a condition for continued enrollment. The policy of a sliding scale of load limits was developed through consultation with the counseling staff and an analysis of student data. The scale parameters and strategy have been regularly reviewed and discussed by counseling faculty. Although this policy was not well received by some students, implementation of this procedure demonstrated that the college values retention and student success, rather than a revolving door.

This policy impacts all students and would therefore affect developmental students, too, who had not been initially subject to the at-risk limits based on their initial assessment results. However, the policy should be considered a first line of defense for a developmental student encountering difficulties after the first semester.

Policy 10: The college provides each student with a mid-term grade progress report. Mid-term grade reports provided students with their direct academic standing for each course in which they were enrolled. Summaries of mid-term reports for tracked, at-risk students' cohorts (including developmental students) were provided to counselors. Mid-term grade reports were used to trigger a number of interventions.

Students whose mid-term projected GPA would place them at some level of academic warning or probation the next semester were required to see a counselor to plan the next term. Such students could not access the early registration system without counselor assistance. In addition, course load restrictions applicable to a student based on the projected GPA were triggered in the computer for early registration.

The college had always maintained a mid-term grading system. The new policy used the data to improve tracking of at-risk students, both developmental and nondevelopmental. The linkage to the registration system allowed proactive intervention for students who were experiencing difficulty in a current semester. In the past, such students would have registered early without linkage to the student success policies.

Policy 11: Mailers detailing academic progress are sent out to all students at the fourth week of each semester. Four-week mailers were generated in conjunction with a computerized attendance report. Each faculty member selected from a menu of ten messages ranging from praise for students doing well to notifications of satisfactory or unsatisfactory progress. The system provided computer-generated letters to the homes of students early in the term, and faculty participation was as easy as completing the Scantron form.

This policy, applicable to developmental as well as nondevelopmental students, should be considered an example of a connecting activity initiated by faculty. Although faculty were not required to participate in the mailing system, a high percentage participated because it was linked to the mandatory state reimbursement attendance verification report.

Policy 12: A degree-audit system details status and advising information to students prior to each subsequent registration. A computer-generated report that advised students on course selection based on their program or educational objective was mailed to students prior to early registration. The degree-audit system also advised developmental students about the next required developmental course. The degree-audit system was accessed through kiosks on campus. The system data could be used by a student for self-advising and by counselors working directly with a student. For at-risk developmental students, the degree-audit system was a proactive but connecting activity that assisted students to effectively plan their schedules to achieve their educational objectives.

The degree-audit system originally focused on specific career associate in applied science degree program requirements and only very general transfer degree program requirements, but it was adapted to provide specific transfer information by specific universities. Potential future enhancements will provide computer-generated information based on specific upper-division *major* requirements. For developmental students with transfer objectives, the degree-audit system provides essential advising information connecting the students to their ultimate educational objectives.

Policy 13: Early identification of the student's educational objective, including the target university for transfer students, is required for all students. All students, both developmental and nondevelopmental, must indicate at each registration their educational intention on the registration form. Student intention identification also became a mandatory element of phone registration. Intention declarations were updated at each registration. Students were required to identify the specific university to which they intended to transfer, and not just indicate a generic "transfer interest."

Following placement testing, students were scheduled to attend a two and one-half hour orientation, which included verification and explanation of educational objectives such as transfer or immediate job preparation.

The educational intention declaration is considered a reinforcing and connecting student success strategy. A specific target involving a named university or a specific job can help motivate students who require developmental education.

Policy 14: All associate in arts or associate in science transfer students or associate in applied science students indicating an intention to transfer are required to develop a Transfer Master Academic Plan. All full-time students intending to transfer, both developmental and nondevelopmental, were required to take a one-credit student success course that developed a Master Academic Plan. The Transfer Master Academic Plan detailed the transfer course curricula a student should follow that fulfilled both the college's general education requirements and those of the intended transfer university. The student signed the plan, which was the basis of the college's transfer guarantee. All part-time students who intended to transfer were also required to develop a Master Academic Plan transfer strategy after completing twelve hours.

Conclusion

The South Suburban College experience demonstrated that it was possible to implement a structured open access system based on the proactive and interventionist philosophies suggested in the retention and student success literature. The system was applicable to all students, including those requiring developmental education. Rather than creating second-class status for developmental and at-risk students, the policies were aimed at connecting and supporting all students equally in the pursuit of their educational objectives. The policies of sorting and transforming students carried out within a supportive and caring environment demonstrated that intrusive and interventionist procedures need not be punitive. On the contrary, such student success strategies are in the finest traditions of community colleges providing genuine access to students and supporting students in a positive fashion to reach their individual educational goals.

References

Beatty-Guenter, P. "Sorting, Supporting, Connecting and Transforming: Retention Strategies at Community Colleges." *Community College Journal of Research and Practice,* 1994, *18* (2), 113–130.

Cohen, A. M., and Brawer, F. B. *The Collegiate Function of Community Colleges: Fostering Higher Learning Through Curriculum and Student Transfer.* San Francisco: Jossey-Bass, 1987.

Eaton, J. S. (ed.). *Colleges of Choice: The Enabling Impact of the Community College.* New York: Macmillan, 1988.

Karabel, J. "Community Colleges and Social Stratification." *Harvard Educational Review,* 1972 *42* (4), 521–562.

Kingan, M. E., and Alfred, R. L. "Entry Assessment in Community Colleges: Tracking or Facilitating?" *Community College Review,* 1993, *21* (3), 3–16.

Lopez, M., Yanez, M., Clayton, E. R., and Thompson, D. A. "Intrusive Advising with Special Student Populations." *NASPA Journal,* 1988, *25* (3), 195–201.

Richardson, R. C. "The Presence of Access and the Pursuit of Achievement." In J. S. Eaton (ed.), *Colleges of Choice: The Enabling Impact of the Community College.* New York: Macmillan, 1988.

Roueche, J. E., and Roueche, S. *Between a Rock and a Hard Place: The At-Risk Student in the Open-Door College.* Washington, D.C.: American Association of Community Colleges, 1993.

Roueche, J. E., and Roueche, S. "Responding to the Challenge of the At-Risk Student." *Community College Journal of Research and Practice,* 1994, *18* (1), 1–11.

RICHARD FONTE is president of Austin Community College and was president of South Suburban College when it initiated the structured open access model.

When Portland Community College was hit with a burgeoning enrollment of non-native English speakers, college staff had to decide whether to increase course sections to accommodate twice as many students as they currently served, or to curtail enrollment and better serve those students who gained admission. This chapter discusses issues involved in the quality/quantity dilemma of providing remedial/developmental English-as-a-second-language programs.

Quality Versus Quantity in the Delivery of Developmental Programs for ESL Students

Reuel Kurzet

In the 1960s community colleges struggled to meet the needs of large numbers of underprepared, first-generation college students. In successfully meeting that challenge, community colleges earned their reputation for providing open-door access to postsecondary education for diverse, nontraditional students. Over the years, the diversity of students has continued to increase. Community colleges are now the schools of choice for homemakers returning to school, laid-off workers retraining for a new career, senior high school students getting a jump-start on college, retirees pursuing leisure education, mid-career workers upgrading their skills, and, increasingly, new immigrants and refugees learning English. It is this last group of students, those with limited English skills, that will likely challenge community colleges most in the coming decades. Taken together, students with limited English skills provide greater diversity of student backgrounds, needs, and goals than any previous group the community college has educated. Their numbers are growing steadily. Will community colleges meet this new challenge?

The New Demand for English as a Second Language

Immigration to the United States is approaching an all-time high. Allen and Turner (1988) cite Immigration and Naturalization Service data showing that legal immigration averaged 570,000 people a year during the 1980s—a rate 30 percent higher than the average for the 1970s. Legislation enacted in 1990 will permit immigration to exceed seven hundred thousand annually throughout the 1990s (Ellis, 1995, p. 26). Although as percentages of the total U.S.

population these numbers lack the impact of the peak immigration decade of 1900–1910, they are nonetheless substantial. According to the U.S. Census Bureau, immigration during the decade of the 1980s accounted for one-quarter to one-third of the nation's population growth (Allen and Turner, 1988, p. 23). "By the year 2000, more than 40 million Americans will be non-native speakers of English . . . [and] almost one-quarter of the new workers in the U.S. labor force will be immigrants" (Thomas, Bird, and Grover, 1992; in Tichenor, 1994, p. 57). Many of these new immigrants will need English language instruction, as well as postsecondary academic and vocational training, to prepare them for productive work and active citizenship in our society. Are community colleges aware of this growing challenge?

In many cases they are not. Because the relatively sudden increase in immigration has caught community colleges by surprise, many have been slow to update either their thinking about English-as-a-second-language (ESL) instruction or their programs for providing it. Historically, ESL instruction was provided by volunteers, often through churches and civic organizations, to enable immigrants to work and participate in community life. The volunteer teachers were not professionally trained; indeed, there was no professional English as a second language discipline. As non- and limited-English-speaking students came to community colleges, programs were set up hastily in various departments of the college, such as English, foreign language, and adult basic education. The location of the ESL program within the college was often determined by the most viable funding source available, rather than through a strictly disciplinary rationale. Some colleges set up several different ESL programs, with different goals, in different departments. The results were as uneven as the programs. Until fairly recently, there were sufficient numbers of low-skilled, family-wage jobs in the United States; those who lacked English proficiency and education could still support their families.

Conditions have changed, of course, for both the immigrants and American business. U.S. companies now believe that they need highly skilled workers to compete in the global economy. Yet "corporate managers often find themselves relying on functionally illiterate and innumerate workers" (Drinane, quoted in Tichenor, 1994, p. 57). Numerous national reports note that U.S. family-wage jobs will increasingly require oral language proficiency, literacy, and numeracy, as well as some postsecondary vocational-technical training.

Most community colleges have yet to rethink how these changing needs will be addressed for their growing numbers of ESL students. Instead, as the number of immigrants rises, community colleges are concerned that the need for ESL instruction and other remediation will overwhelm their primary commitment to lower-division collegiate and vocational-technical degree and certificate programs. Further, community colleges face pressure from declining state revenues and eroding public trust in all levels of education. According to Gary Eaton, president of Maricopa Community College in Mesa, Arizona, community colleges everywhere are expected to do more with less (personal communication, December 16, 1996). These pressures make it difficult for community college leaders to address ESL afresh. Meanwhile, "the delivery of ESL instruction in community colleges is not neat, but slides around the curriculum from college to college and even within an institution" (Ignash, 1995, p. 18). Many ESL students continue to be taught by nonprofessionals, even through ESL has become a growing international professional discipline over the past thirty years. Further, the frequent organizational isolation of ESL faculty and students from the mainstream of the college and its services acts as a barrier to ESL students seeking to matriculate into the college credit and vocational-technical programs they need.

Some community colleges are beginning to meet the challenge. As they become aware of the new demographics and their economic, social, and political implications, educational leaders are reconsidering the delivery of their ESL programs. In cities with large immigrant populations, the chief dilemma is that of "quantity or quality." Community colleges must decide whether to serve increasing numbers of ESL students in traditional ESL programs—with large classes taught by part-time instructors and volunteers, often isolated from the rest of the college—or to focus instead on improving the quality of their ESL programs and support services to encourage limited-English-speaking students to complete their ESL study and matriculate into academic and vocational-technical programs within the college. This single question, whether to emphasize quantity or quality in ESL instruction, can be the basis of a thorough review and restructuring of community college ESL instruction.

The Dilemma at Portland Community College: Balancing Demand with Quality

Portland Community College, in Portland, Oregon, has been grappling with that very question. As is often the case, a crisis precipitated the program's reevaluation. From 1986 to 1991, the increasing numbers of ESL students in the adult education ESL program were served in traditional fashion, with large classes predominantly taught by part-time faculty. The school received generous funding under the amnesty provision of the federal Immigration Reform and Control Act of 1986. In the spring of 1991, however, Portland Community College lost its amnesty funds.

The ESL department acquired its first department chair in June of that year. Her first major assignment was to cut the program from nearly sixty class sections to twenty-six and to lay off an equal number of part-time ESL instructors. Morale and funding were low, but the students were not so easily discouraged. ESL class waiting lists swelled to over eight hundred students. The college's administration continually received calls from English-speaking friends, relatives, and employers of former and hopeful ESL students.

At first, little was done to address the problem. The department chair was new and inexperienced, as was the division dean administrating the program. Eventually a temporary solution was implemented, in a desperate response to the long waiting lists of ESL student hopefuls. The college has a policy of designating surplus funds at the end of the fiscal year as rollover contingency funds for the next fiscal year. A generous portion of these funds has been allocated to the ESL department for each of the past two years to add more ESL class sections. These efforts to address the quantity of ESL have had mixed results. Students quickly have filled any extra class sections opened. The college has benefited from the increase in state reimbursements. Some of the students learned a substantial amount of English during the three terms that contingency dollars permitted them to study. Yet each year, the funds ran out before the next allocation of contingency money could reinstate the classes. The cycle of growth and decline was difficult for everyone involved.

Until 1993, the ESL department had only three full-time faculty, one of whom was also the department chair. All three felt overburdened with the demands of continuously recruiting, hiring, training, and then laying off part-time instructors; finding, opening, and then closing class sites; and conducting other operational tasks related to the continual, budget-driven cycle of expansion and contraction. Finally, the full-time faculty decided to get involved in program planning. Their division dean, although retaining the authority to make final decisions, agreed to delegate much of the program planning responsibility to the department chair and full-time faculty. The full-time ESL faculty's initial goal was to press for financial stability for the program. Gradually, they became involved in additional efforts that addressed not only the level of funding, or the quantity of ESL, but also quality concerns. Although faculty in the ESL department would agree that much still needs to be done to improve both the quantity and the quality of ESL instruction at the college, much progress has been made in the past several years.

The fluctuating program size and resulting instability led to low morale and high turnover among the part-time faculty. The ESL department chair sought to improve part-time faculty morale and improve program quality while reducing student and staff attrition. Together with other full- and part-time ESL faculty, the ESL department chair took a number of steps to address these issues.

Several part-time positions were created that provided valued support to part-time instructors. An experienced part-time instructor was paid to provide orientation to all new part-time faculty. That gave new part-time instructors an immediate link with another part-time faculty member. The same part-time instructor was also paid to maintain and keep current an extensive collection of carefully prepared and edited teacher-made classroom materials. These materials filled fourteen file cabinets and were organized systematically in relation to the ESL department's adult education curricula.

Because ESL classes were held at numerous on- and off-campus locations, most without any full-time support, an experienced part-time instructor at each site was paid to be the site leader. Site leaders served as ESL department liaisons with the building manager for their site, the main ESL office's clerical staff, and the ESL department chair to ensure that sufficient office and instructional supplies were provided and classrooms were clean and comfortable. The overall goal was to provide adequate instructional support, so that instructors could focus on teaching.

Another important new position was that of level leader. Each of the four instructional levels in the ESL program had a paid, experienced, part-time faculty level leader who provided course-specific orientation for newly hired instructors and for instructors new to teaching that level. At quarterly level meetings, experienced instructors shared materials and successful teaching ideas with each other and with new instructors of that level. This developed a departmental faculty norm of sharing successful classroom ideas and materials and of supporting rather than competing against one another.

ESL full-time and part-time faculty members considered themselves one faculty. This was unusual. In many community college departments the full-time faculty do not even know the names of all of the part-time faculty. The ESL department held an annual holiday pot-luck for all faculty and their partners. Some years, a summer picnic was held as well. These informal activities encouraged ESL faculty friendships and general collegiality.

The college had provided voice mail boxes for the faculty for many years, but the ESL department was the first to assign voice mail boxes to all of its part-time instructors and to set up a distribution list allowing any ESL instructor to leave a message for all ESL instructors simultaneously. This had obvious value for routine administrative announcements. It also enabled part-time faculty members to easily request a substitute instructor if they were ill, to share information about ESL job openings in the metropolitan area, and to share teaching tips and queries. Additionally, about one-third of the part-time ESL instructors had an E-mail account at the college.

These were all small steps, but collectively they had a positive influence on the ESL faculty. Morale improved and attrition declined. Part-time faculty turnover for the past three years has been about ten percent per year. Most importantly, ESL students benefited from having a committed staff of experienced ESL instructors.

The other side of providing high-quality support to ESL instructors is to expect that they will, in turn, provide high-quality instruction to ESL students. The full-time ESL faculty worked with the human resources department to develop an equitable screening and hiring procedure that included a thorough forty-minute interview to assess each applicant's ability to apply his or her professional ESL training to the kinds of students served by our program. Once hired, new instructors received the program, site, and course-level orientations mentioned above. New instructors received both a self-observation checklist and a copy of the ESL department's teacher observation form. The latter was the same form that was used to assess instructors' teaching effectiveness during classroom observations. It listed the criteria for assessment and thus provided new instructors with very specific ESL program expectations.

The teacher observation form was developed by the three original full-time ESL faculty members. Without exception, every instructor in the ESL department had the opportunity to veto any proposed item that he or she thought inappropriate for assessing ESL instruction. As a result, the teacher observation instrument enjoyed full acceptance as a valid assessment instrument of effective instruction within the ESL department. Care was taken to specify research-supported criteria of effective ESL and adult education instructional practices without infringing on academic freedom.

To ensure that new instructors were covered by the new policies, they were observed in the classroom by one of the four full-time instructors during their first term working in the ESL department. If their teaching was substantially below program standards, they were not rehired. Careful screening and interviewing means that this outcome is rare. Teachers whose skills marginally meet program standards but who appear to have potential are assigned to work with a teaching mentor. The mentor helps the new instructor with lesson plans, observes his or her class once every two weeks, and provides formative evaluation feedback. One of the four full-time instructors returns to observe the instructor again the following term. To be offered further teaching assignments, the new instructor must fully meet program quality standards by the third term. This same mentoring program is available to experienced instructors who are teaching a new course for the first time or who are dealing with personal or family emergencies that negatively affect their teaching.

Staff development money, provided by the state, has allowed both full-time and part-time instructors to attend local and regional professional conferences, such as ORTESOL, the Oregon affiliate of the international professional association, Teachers of English to Speakers of Other Languages. Staff development money has also been used to pay part-time instructors to participate in peer observations as well as curriculum and materials development projects. These activities support on-going faculty professional development but also establish expectations for instructors to participate professionally outside the classroom.

In addition to addressing the quality of ESL instruction, another major effort was undertaken to enhance the quality of services ESL students received at the college. Historically, from the ESL program's inception, all new ESL students were tested and registered by ESL instructors. At the beginning of each term, placement testing was conducted at each site where classes were offered. To reserve limited funds for classroom instruction, each site had only two to four part-time instructors to test, place, advise, and either register or turn away prospective students. As many as 260 students typically appeared on open testing and registration days. Many students were placed into classes, but many others were turned away. Poor test security and inadequate student advising were serious problems. The faculty felt that drastic changes needed to be made.

The ESL department chair initiated an effort to bring ESL students firmly into the mainstream of the college. That was a major change for the institution because ESL students had always been handled separately from regular college procedures and services. It took a three-year effort and an ESL-led cross-functional team with representatives from testing, admissions, registration, management information systems, and administration to effect the highly successful change. Now all prospective ESL students make an appointment for placement testing at the college testing office on any campus. Only twenty to twenty-five students are tested at one time. Each student receives individual advising from a part-time ESL faculty member and is given assistance, if necessary, in filling out the college registration form. ESL students go through the same registration procedure as all other college students. During the registration process, ESL students also receive college identification cards that enable them to use the library, athletic, and other college facilities.

Another improvement in student services for ESL students is that now each student has a noncredit transcript generated that shows the student's ESL course history. Students find these noncredit transcripts useful in obtaining employment or work promotions. Other efforts to improve college services to ESL students are still in progress. They include improved counseling services, access to college language and developmental education labs, better access and improved assessment services from the Office for Students with Disabilities, and better access to classroom space for ESL on the campuses. These steps, which begin to integrate ESL students into the college mainstream, facilitate students' later entry into college credit academic and vocational-technical programs. The students appreciate that they are now being recognized as "real" students and take their studies seriously.

Documented results show that efforts to improve the quality of ESL instruction are worthwhile. Retention in the noncredit ESL department for the past two years, since the changes were initiated, has averaged over 87 percent. Two of Portland Community College's three campuses that have advanced ESL programs, called ENL, reported that two-thirds of their new students are former ESL students. The third campus reported that half of its new ENL students were from ESL. (That campus also had many younger students entering ENL directly from high school.) Strong student enrollment and retention in ESL courses has also benefited the college financially by providing increased reimbursable FTE (full-time student equivalent funding).

The Future: Policy Recommendations for Continuing Quality Concerns

In spite of these important quality improvements in Portland Community College's ESL program, the struggle for stable funding to serve the growing number of prospective ESL students continues. The state's voters recently passed a property tax limitation that will reduce the college's operating budget by nearly 10 percent over the next two years. With even the best of intentions, it will be difficult for the administration to maintain the ESL department's current level of funding, much less to increase funds. For now, the ESL department provides a smooth registration process, expanded student services, and improved quality of instruction for those who successfully gain entry into the program. Contingency funds have allowed the program to increase its course sections by nearly 25 percent over the past two years. Those funds will run out in two terms. The struggle to improve both the quality and quantity of ESL will go on.

Although the problem of providing high-quality ESL instruction to growing numbers of limited-English speakers in our society is not amenable to an easy solution, it is an issue that community college leaders everywhere need to revisit. If projections are correct and current trends continue, there will be no majority culture or race in the United States by the middle of the twenty-first century (Riche, cited in Ellis 1995, p. 26). The new community college student may soon be a non-native speaker of English. Declining enrollments of traditional students mean that community colleges will benefit from encouraging non-native speakers to complete ESL and enter the transfer and vocational-technical programs they need for future careers.

Addressing the need to improve and expand ESL offerings in community colleges will not be easy. Three major impediments are a lack of understanding of who ESL students are and what they need, outdated assumptions about ESL instruction and student services, and scarce public funding for education.

A significant impediment to improving the quality of ESL instruction is the widespread misconception by those who make decisions about community college ESL programs of who ESL students are. Current management literature for education emphasizes that knowing one's students and their needs is essential to providing quality education (Marchese 1991, p. 4). Who are ESL students? What is their background? What do they need and want from community colleges?

Often ESL students are defined by the community college's placement of its ESL instruction. For example, the provision of ESL through an adult education program may lead to the assumption that the ESL students are illiterate or marginally literate adult education students. That definition describes some of the students in the program, but it fails to recognize that the prior education of ESL students ranges from primary schooling through university and professional school. Students have widely varying needs and goals. Programs set up on the adult basic education model, for example, poorly meet the needs of highly educated professionals who simply do not speak English. Assuming that the placement of the ESL department accurately describes the population served is a serious error; usually it is the funding source for the ESL program that determines its location within a community college. To serve students well, and especially to track them into appropriate academic and vocational-technical training programs, it is essential to know who the individual students are and what they need and want.

Another impediment to quality is the common practice of hiring instructors qualified to teach in adult basic education literacy programs, usually anyone with a college degree, as ESL instructors. This error also stems from the misconception of who ESL students are. ESL instructors need solid preparation in English linguistics, second language acquisition, intercultural communication, and effective language teaching methods. This preparation can be found in graduates of professional teaching English as a second language (TESL) programs or applied linguistics programs, or graduates of related programs, such as English or foreign languages, who have supplemented their programs with TESL training.

Having appropriately trained, professional instructors, including at least some full-time professional staff, makes a measurable difference in program quality and student outcomes. The National Evaluation of Adult Education Programs, an extensive study funded by the U.S. Department of Education, found that having some professional full-time staff, at least one administrator, and at least one full-time professional instructor was an important predictor of student persistence in ESL. Yet only 73 (56 percent) of the 131 programs studied met this minimum requirement for professional, full-time staff (Young, Flieshman, and Fitzgerald, 1992, p. 45).

An impediment to expanding ESL programs to meet the growing need is that community college decision makers may not be completely aware of the funding stream and the costs and benefits of their ESL programs. Money may be available to increase both quantity and quality of ESL instruction—and the ESL program may be providing it. For example, Portland Community College's adult education ESL program makes a substantial profit from its state-reimbursable enrollment, but this is not widely known within the college. States vary in their provision of potential funding for ESL. Some provide funding through the federal Adult Education Act. Others count reimbursable FTE (full-time enrollment) for ESL in the same way as enrollment in transfer programs. Many community colleges would benefit from advocating for increased ESL funding to serve their growing immigrant populations. Funds also may be available through the new federal welfare reform programs as well as through partnerships with businesses.

Instead of fearing that the demand for ESL will take over the mission to provide transfer and vocational-technical education, community colleges can learn to enhance and facilitate ESL students' rapid acquisition of English and matriculation into college transfer and vocational-technical programs. Community colleges should provide ESL students with access to regular student services: appropriate language skills assessment, class placement, and advising. Student learning should be measured and their progress tracked and documented. Links must be established between ESL and other programs within the college. ESL programs must provide professionally trained instructors, increase the number of full-time staff, and ensure that their ESL curriculum and instruction are designed to meet students' needs and goals.

Community colleges everywhere need to step up to the challenge of fully incorporating ESL students into their colleges. Community colleges need ESL students. Our increasingly multicultural workforce certainly needs their skills. It is not enough for community colleges to continue to offer a few overcrowded ESL courses taught by poorly supported and inadequately trained part-time faculty. ESL students need the kinds of quality programs and support services that will encourage them not only to persist in their English studies but also to earn the associate degree or vocational-technical certificate they will need to be productive citizens and workers in our multicultural, global economy.

References

Allen, J. P., and Turner, E. J. "Where to Find the New Immigrants." *American Demographics,* Sep. 1988, pp. 23–27, 59.

Ellis, P. "Language Minority Students: Are Community Colleges Meeting the Challenge?" *Community College Journal,* 1995, *65,* 26–33.

Ignash, J. M. "Encouraging ESL Student Persistence: The Influence of Policy on Curricular Design." *Community College Review,* 1995, *23,* 17–34.

Marchese, T. "TQM Reaches the Academy." *AAHE Bulletin,* 1991, *44* (3), 3–9.

Riche, M. F. "We're All Minorities Now." *American Demographics,* Oct. 1991. Reprinted. *Hispanic Americans,* reprint package 363. Ithaca, N.Y.: American Demographics, 1992.

Tichenor, S. "Community Colleges and Teaching English as a Second Language: Serving the Limited English Proficient." *Community College Review,* 1994, *22,* 55–66.

Thomas, R. J., Bird, L. A., and Grover, J. "Serving Vocational ESL Students." Washington, D.C.: American Association of Community Colleges, 1992. (ED 350 052)

Young, M., Flieshman, H., and Fitzgerald, M. "National Evaluation of Adult Education Programs." Arlington, Virginia: Development Associates, Inc., 1992.

REUEL KURZET is chair of the ESL Department at Portland Community College in Portland, Oregon.

This chapter describes a successful collaboration between high school and community college faculty to reduce the need for remediation in the writing of entering community college students. After participating in Ohio's Early English Composition Assessment Program, which addresses access and preparation of students for college, the authors describe the model they used that led to three years of successful collaboration, outline future efforts, and make recommendations.

Community College/High School Feedback and Collaboration: Preventive Measures

Deborah K. Richey, Jeanette Mathern, Carol S. O'Shea, Shelby J. Pierce

In April of 1981, the Advisory Commission on Articulation Between Secondary Education and Ohio Colleges, appointed jointly by the Ohio Board of Regents and the State Board of Education, published a report on the status of graduating high school students' math and writing skills. Among the conclusions reached by this commission were that graduating high school students lacked basic math and writing skills necessary for them to be fully successful in college entry-level courses and that these students also were deficient in critical thinking, analytical, and problem-solving skills. One reason proposed for these deficiencies was that the high school curriculum was not adequate in preparing students for college-level work; however, the consultants to the commission noted that simply tinkering with the high school curriculum would not solve the problem. In trying to propose recommendations, the commission postulated that the problem was a result of confusion on the part of the high schools in deciding the nature and level of college entry-level skills students should master; indeed, "With notable and praiseworthy exceptions, no formal, systematic communication network exists to ensure that educational institutions at all levels communicate their expectations for incoming students" (Ohio Board of Regents, 1981, p. 6). As a result, one of the eight recommendations of the committee was for "colleges and schools [to] establish formal faculty communication links with one another for articulation purposes." One of the outgrowths of that recommendation by the commission was the Early English Composition Assessment Program (EECAP), initiated in 1984 by the Ohio Board of Regents under the auspices of the Ohio General Assembly.

The Communications/Humanities Department at Owens Community College has been actively involved in EECAP since 1988. The worthwhile projects undertaken during this time period resulted in positive communication among high school and college faculty alike. However, it was the Owens Community College/Findlay High School project implemented in 1994, more ambitious in scope than the other projects, that resulted in the most successful partnership. The project design fostered a strong positive rapport among the faculty members, a mutual understanding of high school English writing requirements and college-level writing requirements and expectations, and a liaison that strengthened comunication. According to the Ohio Board of Regents (1988), EECAP has two purposes: to identify high school students' writing strengths and weaknesses in order that the high schools may intervene prior to student enrollment in college, and to facilitate strong liaisons between high school and college faculty so that a communication bridge is constructed. It was the hope of the initial commission and of the Ohio Board of Regents that if these goals were met, (1) students' strengths would be enhanced and their weaknesses remediated in their later high school years, lessening the need for remediation at the college level, and (2) the positive relationships formed among faculties would result in a continual communication of standards and expectations.

Keeping the above purposes and goals in mind, in 1994, Dr. Carol O'Shea, in collaboration with Findlay High School faculty, designed a proposal for an EECAP grant. This proposal incorporated elements of direct collaboration between college and high school faculty, writing process theory, and portfolio evaluation theory. The overall goal of the project was to improve the writing competencies of Findlay High School students in order to better prepare them for collegiate writing. The Owens and Findlay team believed, however, that with the incorporation of process techniques in the development of "final display" portfolios, students would not only see their writing improve but also be better writers who would understand the nature of writing as a process. They would learn to employ process techniques effectively in their writing, whether it be for college or for career. A second but equally important goal of this project, as advocated by the Ohio Board of Regents, was to foster collaboration between high school and college faculties and administrations. Congenial relationships between high school and college faculty facilitate the process of collaborating about evaluation and assessment issues that affect students' progress from the high school environment to college or the world of work. The Findlay/Owens team valued this goal and worked to bring it to fruition. The following pages describe the nature of this successful collaboration. Specifically addressed are project design, portfolio assessment, and collaboration results and recommendations from the high school teachers' perspectives.

The Collaborative Process and Design of the Project

As a consequence of the open-endedness of the request for proposals, Early English Composition Assessment Program projects vary markedly across the state. Projects planners are given the freedom to design EECAP activities that not only are theoretically valid but also have been customized to meet both short- and long-term practical needs of specific institutions and their students. Some projects may be simple, such as jointly developing a grading rubric, whereas others may be quite complex. However, the necessary first ingredient when designing a purposeful and successful project is rich collaboration between the secondary and postsecondary institutions involved. In fact, it could be said that collaborative conversation across the secondary and post-secondary boundary is the main point of EECAP, with growth in student writing abilities being the desired consequence of collaboration.

Thus, when Findlay High School and Owens Community College faculty agreed to work together on an EECAP proposal, everyone approached the first planning meeting with an open mind. The first objective of each of the two faculties was to learn about the programs, students, and student writing abilities at the other institution. Like so many institutions participating in new EECAP projects, we soon realized that we knew much less than we thought we knew about one another's methods, expectations, and challenges. Through these frank conversations, the disparate views of different faculty members began to gel. We soon recognized a shared value—both institutions preferred that the project take a comprehensive and systemic approach, whatever that might be, rather than isolate a single class level or program feature (such as a rubric). Acknowledging the energy and dedication a complex project would entail, participating faculty and administrators at Findlay High School and Owens Community College began to design their project through a series of meetings.

Although EECAP primarily intends its projects to involve students in their junior year of high school, Findlay High School and Owens Community College participants agreed that involving students at all four grade levels would allow identification of need earlier in the student's high school career and increase the number of opportunities for intervention. We also recognized the potential benefit to participating teachers. Through a faculty development component, the project could help participating writing teachers become more knowledgeable about levels they did not normally teach, giving them a fuller sense of the skills needed at different academic levels (freshman, sophomore, junior, senior, college) so that students advancing from one grade to another could experience a seamless progression through high school and on to college. With all this in mind, we planned our project to include several key components.

One Collaboratively Developed Full-Process Writing Assignment for Each High School Grade Level. Complete with a suggested lesson plan and all required materials, such as supplemental readings, an assignment would be completed by all students in a grade level at roughly the same point in their academic year. Because of the scope of planning needed for this component, we adopted a two-year cycle for the project. We developed materials for the freshman and junior year assignments in the first year of our cycle, and for the sophomore and senior levels in the second year of our cycle. In the third and subsequent years, all four levels were fully active. These assignments were designed to be appropriate for their grade level and anticipatory of the skills needed in future grade levels. Committed to a process approach to writing, the planners agreed that several class sessions would be dedicated to working through the process of each assignment, with the students discussing and preparing in small groups and with their class as a whole. Writing for the assignment was to take place both in and out of class.

Personal Experience Essay (Freshmen). Freshmen were assigned to write a personal experience essay that advised current eighth graders about the skills needed to succeed at Findlay High School. Thesis, basic organizational patterns, simple transitions, development through illustration and example, and strategies for simple introductions and conclusions were stressed in this assignment. To make this activity clearly purposeful, the high school published sample responses in a magazine distributed to current eighth graders.

Process Essay (Sophomores). Sophomores were asked to describe a process in detail. Chronological order, temporal indicators and transitions, and anticipation of an audience's needs and expectations were among the points stressed in this assignment.

Comparison/Contrast Essay with Informal Citation (Juniors). Juniors were taught techniques for organizing purposeful comparison or contrast essays, including alternating and divided patterns and more sophisticated coherence techniques. Critical thinking skills were stressed, as were analysis, audience awareness, and higher-level strategies for special-purpose paragraphs. Students were required to informally integrate and cite at least one source.

Synthesis Argument with Formal Documentation (Seniors). Seniors were required to analyze several source documents and respond to a given topic with a position paper (three to five typewritten pages) that effectively and formally integrated material from their readings. Again, critical thinking was emphasized, as were many argument strategies (concession, qualification, common ground, logical fallacy, and so on).

A Collaboratively Developed Holistic Writing Assessment Tool. Although individual teachers were free to use the assignment however they preferred in grading their courses, for the purposes of the project a shared holistic assessment tool was developed. The tool provided descriptors for five different levels of overall performance, ranked from zero to four.

A Collaboratively Developed Training Module for Participating Faculty. To prepare teachers for teaching the assignments and to prepare readers for assessing student responses to the assignments, planners worked together to create a training packet for each grade level that explained the assignment and provided explanations of assessments and samples for reader practice and norming. Readers (Findlay High School English teachers and Owens Community College participating faculty and administrators) gathered for training prior to reading and through practice and discussion reached impressively consistent consensus on assessment standards and decisions.

A Collaborative Assessment System. Each piece of student writing was holistically read and scored by at least two readers, who compared their assessments after scoring. If they agreed in their assessment, the score was recorded. If they disagreed, they discussed their thinking and attempted to reach agreement. In rare instances when agreement was not forthcoming, a third reader may have been invited to read the piece. After assessment decisions were reached, feedback was recorded for the student author's benefit. Combined training and assessment sessions usually took six to eight hours, given the number of students enrolled.

A Portfolio Component. To ensure that teachers and students had access to longitudinal information about each writer's skill development, the planning team designed a portfolio component. The portfolio, which could contain other samples of writing in addition to the EECAP assignments, was maintained at the school throughout the student's high school career, easily accessible to instructors and individual student authors for periodic review and discussion. The portfolios were given to their student authors at the end of their senior year for college placement or other purposes.

It would be inaccurate to imply that our design sprang from our discussions full-formed and flawless. Every component of the project was revised and adjusted in an evolving effort. Perhaps nowhere was this more true than in the portfolio component. A more detailed examination of that component follows.

Portfolio Assessment Collaboration

The Findlay High School/Owens Community College EECAP portfolio project is still in its infancy. Every phase of the portfolio project began with a research team of EECAP participants from Owens Community College and Findlay High School who gathered information to share with the entire EECAP team. Initially, the 1994–95 sessions concentrated on current portfolio methodology, rubric models, portfolio logistics, and ways to introduce the portfolios to the students. In the two subsequent years, the Owens Community College/Findlay High School team discussed the contents of the portfolio, refined the logistics process, and evaluated a portion of the student portfolios. In the last year of the project, 1997–98, the team will focus on assessing the senior portfolios.

First-Year Portfolio Activities. Portfolio methodology research involved several Findlay High School and two Owens faculty members. The research team met between the scheduled EECAP sessions to compare information, determine what still needed to be researched, and design the agenda for the next four EECAP sessions. The group investigated the literature on portfolios and selected a definition of the portfolio based on the work of Susan Cramer. In "Navigating the Assessment Maze with Portfolios," Cramer describes the portfolio as "a collection of student work that documents the process of learning and individual growth" (Cramer, 1993, p. 72). The need to show process and document growth was necessary for Findlay High School faculty to have a history of all students in order to address individual writing problems from the start.

Elizabeth Metzger and Lizbeth Bryant (1993) believe that the portfolio provides the students the "opportunity to become 'real experienced' writers. Real writers have many opportunities to revise. . . . Real world writers also interact with others to develop their ideas and their texts" (p. 285). The EECAP team especially liked what Metzger and Bryant had to say because an important component of the writing assignments was to provide as real an audience as possible to motivate the students. The portfolio not only provided us with the opportunity to learn about students' writing but also provided students with an opportunity to learn about themselves as writers. Pat Belanoff and Marcia Dickson (1991) note that "portfolios are particularly appropriate vehicles for metacognitive awareness. Both students and teachers can see a term's work and can hardly resist reflecting on what has happened over a period of weeks" (p. xxiii). A major purpose of the EECAP assignments and portfolios was to provide motivation for all students, but especially for those students who did not see college as an option, whether because of lack of self-esteem, parental or teacher encouragement, or ability. Hopefully, students would be able to see growth throughout each school year as well as the cumulative four years of high school, providing incentive for further education or at least increased self-esteem.

The group then designed a rubric for the portfolio that evaluated growth and identified weaknesses in writing. The rubric also needed to be easy for the instructors to use. Group members presented many writing assessment rubrics. A rubric that Elbow (1993) uses as an example in "Ranking, Evaluating, and Liking" provided a good starting point. The group designed a rubric that contained three columns labeled Strong, OK, and Weak. (No failing grades are given on portfolios.) The rubric also included a section for faculty comments. The portfolio provided the student with a guide for improvement, and the next year's teacher with an immediate history of the student's work.

Next, the group discussed the logistics of handling the portfolios. A Findlay High School faculty member presented a plan for handling the portfolios the first year, knowing that storage equipment would be needed the following year.

To introduce the portfolios to students, teams of group members presented various lesson plans and used the best components from each of the different presentations. For instance, one exemplary lesson plan used portfolios in different art fields, with examples of the student's attempts with different media, best work, and works in progress. When the portfolios were introduced to the students, the following items were addressed: a definition and model of a portfolio, student benefits of using portfolios, a bring-share-reflect assignment, the concepts of ownership and student self-evaluation, and the types of assignments that could be placed in the portfolio.

The first year ended with a sample evaluation of some of the freshman and junior student portfolios. A review of students' prewriting suggested that they attempted innovative approaches to the EECAP assignments, but these ideas never surfaced in the final drafts. What did appear was not original, but perfunctory. Some students also did not revise as much as their teachers had suggested. These examples provided necessary feedback for the Findlay High School faculty.

Second-Year Portfolio Activities. In the second year, the group determined the content of the portfolio. The Findlay High School faculty and students had considerable flexibility in choosing assignments for the portfolio, although the portfolios had to contain self-reflection questions and a letter from the student to the following year's teacher discussing the portfolio. The group also refined the logistics process, adding a working portfolio, which contained everything the student did throughout the year, and a showcase portfolio, which contained only what was to be evaluated. At the end of the second year, the team evaluated a portion of the student portfolios as a group as a norming activity. The Findlay High School faculty evaluated their own portfolios and consulted another Findlay High School reader if necessary.

Third- and Fourth-Year Portfolio Activities. At the end of project year 1996–97, some Findlay High School faculty members shared their portfolios and how they evaluated them, using the portfolio rubric. At the end of the fourth year, the group will concentrate solely on the senior portfolios to assess the progress of the students as writers, evaluate the portfolio process itself, and revise the rubric to make it more user-friendly, if warranted.

The portfolio project at this point has excited the Findlay High School faculty. Other Findlay High School faculty not on the EECAP team have provided valuable feedback concerning assignments and student comments throughout the project. Working together has engendered a feeling of community between the two schools' faculties. The knowledge the two groups have shared concerning the teaching and assessment of writing has proven invaluable.

The High School Teachers' Perspective

Although the mission was a noble one, the project was not easy for the high school English department. The results have been worthwhile, however, even though the process was messy. The faculty are just beginning to see the benefits of the EECAP project to students.

A major reason for the success of the project has been the diplomacy and genuineness of the Owens Community College faculty. The community college faculty were serious, well prepared, and sincerely interested in helping Findlay High School teachers. Never did they appear condescending. At meetings, both responsibility and input were shared and decisions were democratically made. There was no sense that a "higher level" faculty had come to straighten out "lower level" teachers.

Another critical component for success has been the willingness of the high school faculty to accept suggestions for change. They were largely open to new ideas and eager to try even the more difficult, elaborate schemes if they held the promise of long-term benefits to students. The high school faculty members were also secure enough in their subject-area knowledge and professional integrity not to be threatened by suggestions from the community college faculty. Respect and appreciation was present from the onset, and through the process faculty have become friends and colleagues.

The difficulty, from a high school teacher's perspective, had more to do with the logistics of such a project. It began with the full schedule of meetings. For the first two years, the committee of six met with the Owens Community College Communications faculty for twelve half-day sessions a year. Each spring, the entire department of seventeen also met for two full-day grading sessions. In addition, each committee member had homework assignments and subcommittee meetings before each half-day session to create lesson plans and collect research. The time commitment for the committee members was almost overwhelming in the first two design years.

The high school teachers also had to sell the idea to their students. In the wake of state high school proficiency standards that sometimes do not have a bearing on passing a grade level or graduating from high school, high school students have become cynical and suspicious of any kind of systemwide writing sample and do not hesitate to ask for explanations. Teachers spent considerable time responding to students' demands for explanations before they accepted the project. An additional challenge was to work the essays into the existing syllabus as naturally as possible.

The following fall, the high school faculty realized how difficult the portfolios were to manage. New file cabinets were needed in most rooms, and finding funds for them was difficult. An even more difficult task, however, was the end-of-the-year chore of sorting the portfolios for the next year's teachers. High school participants in the EECAP project frequently spent additional hours after school to perform EECAP-related chores.

Even with all the difficulties, however, benefits have been real. The high school English department has gained consistency in teaching and evaluating student writing. In addition, it has raised the level of instruction in writing for the so-called general student by virtue of comparing all students of a grade level on the same 0–4 scale in the spring of each year. Although teachers of non-college-bound students resisted the "unfairness" of this comparison in early meetings, they later agreed to the new standards because, in the long run, students are better prepared for college-bound writing tasks.

Receiving the previous year's portfolios in the fall has also aided new teachers in assessing individual student writing needs. By a quick glance at the cover sheet on the portfolio a teacher can see in September that someone needs "depth of content" or "proofreading help." Months are not lost assessing a student's proficiency level and what he or she needs. EECAP has forced a kind of pragmatic record-keeping that the high school faculty have always wanted but did not have the mechanism to develop or implement on their own.

For the student, having the portfolio means that teachers know and care what they can write and what they have written. They see the thread that connects writing instruction across the four years. They themselves can be reminded in September of the areas that still need work. Also, evaluating and selecting the portfolio pieces are valuable exercises in themselves.

Conclusions and Recommendations

This collaboration worked because of the dedication of both the community college and the high school team members to their profession, the warm interpersonal relationships that developed, and the willingness of team members to prepare for sessions and to work hard. Similar collaborative projects should consider the following recommendations:

Start on a small scale. Begin by achieving administrative support, but bring the actual participants together soon and involve them in the planning of the project.

Involve as many people from the departments as possible. The collaborative workshop element of this project was the key to fostering a cooperative relationship. The program was a shared effort—not one group dictating to another. In addition, for the project to be successful, everyone must feel that he or she can provide feedback that will be heard.

Keep communication lines open with those not directly involved with the project. The problems that did arise in this project resulted from participants forgetting to promptly and clearly communicate with or request input from faculty and administrative personnel from both institutions who were not part of the EECAP project group.

Expect to work hard. As participants in this project, the high school faculty increased their workload by adding new writing assignments and a portfolio assessment element to their curriculum. They also spent time outside the normal school day preparing for the workshops and assessment days.

Evaluate the project every year, asking for input from all involved—including the students. Many excellent suggestions resulted from those evaluations.

The effort involved in such a collaboration is daunting, and the commitment of time and resources is formidable. History and experience have revealed that without the high level of administrative and faculty commitment and cooperation that were in evidence at Owens Community College and Findlay High School, programs like this can languish. If programs like EECAP are carefully planned, objectives clearly set, timelines zealously adhered to, and cooperation jointly nourished, success is inevitable. Without minimizing what the faculties and administrators realize from such cooperative ventures, students are the principal benefactors. They can take away insights into the writing process, obviously, and lessons about college writing expectations and evaluations. More importantly, they begin to approach their writing with more confidence and conviction, and with a greater sense that writing can help define who they are and what they want in life.

References

Belanoff, P., and Dickson, M. (eds.). *Portfolios: Process and Product.* Portsmouth, N.H.: Boyton/Cook, 1991.

Cramer, S. R. "Navigating the Assessment Maze with Portfolios." *The Clearing House,* 1993, 67 (2), 72–74.

Elbow, P. "Ranking, Evaluating, and Liking: Sorting Out Three Forms of Judgment." *College English,* 1993, 55 (2), 187–206.

Metzger, E., and Bryant, L. "Portfolio Assessment: Pedagogy, Power, and the Student." *TETYC,* 1993, 20, 278–288.

Ohio Board of Regents. *Early English Composition Assessment Program Request for Proposals.* Columbus: Ohio Board of Regents, 1988.

Ohio Board of Regents. *Report: Advisory Commission on Articulation Between Secondary Education and Ohio Colleges.* Columbus: Ohio Board of Regents, State Board of Education, 1981.

DEBORAH K. RICHEY is assistant professor in the Communications/Humanities Department at Owens Community College, Toledo, Ohio.   ·

JEANETTE MATHERN is a faculty member in the English Department at Findlay High School, Findlay, Ohio.

CAROL S. O'SHEA is assistant professor in the Communications/Humanities Department at Owens Community College, Toledo, Ohio.

SHELBY J. PIERCE is chair of the Communications/Humanities Department at Owens Community College, Toledo, Ohio.

*How do we know if a college's remedial/developmental programs are
effective in remediating students? Evaluation should go beyond simply
determining whether courses are effective and should examine the
placement of students, the timing of remediation, and the eventual
student enrollment in college-level courses as measures of effectiveness.*

Using Research to Evaluate
Developmental Education
Programs and Policies

Julie Weissman, Carole Bulakowski, Marci K. Jumisko

The United States has long been proud of its egalitarian traditions, infused also
into its system of higher education. Concerns about access have been the driving force behind many of the higher education policies developed at federal,
state, and local levels. Educators admitting students at Harvard in the 1600s
faced the challenge of providing access to those college students who needed
additional help to meet academic standards (Keimig, 1983). That challenge
has continued for three hundred years and still poses a dilemma for educators
who face increasing demands from parents, employers, and taxpayers who per-
ceive that the quality of higher education is declining. Colleges have responded
to this challenge by developing multiple types of courses and academic support systems for underprepared students to help them succeed in pursuing
their academic goals.

A recent document from the National Center for Education Statistics,
Remedial Education at Higher Education Institutions in Fall 1995 (USDE, 1996),
reports that 78 percent of higher education institutions that enrolled freshmen
offered at least one developmental education course in fall 1995. Of the community colleges surveyed for the study, 100 percent offered developmental
education courses, 99 percent offering courses in all three skill areas (reading,
writing, and math). According to the report, 41 percent of first-time freshmen
at community colleges enrolled in at least one developmental education reading, writing, or math course in fall 1995. Given the extent of community college involvement in developmental education, the question remains, are these
programs effective?

A well-designed developmental education program must include a strong evaluation component. Demands for accountability, especially those directed toward publicly funded community colleges, suggest that program evaluation should be a routine activity of institutions offering developmental education courses and activities. Yet a study of 116 two- and four-year institutions revealed that only a small percentage conducted any systematic evaluation of their developmental education programs (Boylan, Bonham, and Bliss, 1994). After further analysis, the authors of this study concluded, "the presence of a regular and systematic evaluation component characterizes the more successful developmental programs" (p. 6).

Evaluation of a developmental education program is critical because it will reveal if the program is accomplishing its purpose, if the students are succeeding, and if the policies the institution has put in place are facilitating student success. Without evaluation, it is impossible to tell which components of a program are working and what needs to be changed. Evaluation should go beyond determining if the courses are effective. It should also examine the policies the college has established to govern the developmental education program, including placement, the timing of remediation, and enrollment in college-level courses.

Decision making about the effectiveness of a program and the policies governing the program should be grounded in research. Collaboration among developmental education faculty and staff and the college's institutional research staff will result in stronger programs and policies that integrate theory and practice with research.

Assessing Effectiveness

The purpose of developmental education is to enable students to gain the skills necessary to complete college-level courses and academic programs successfully. To assess the effectiveness of a program, several outcomes should be examined: (1) Do students complete developmental education successfully? (2) Do students move from developmental education to college-level courses? (3) Are students who have taken remedial/developmental courses completing college-level courses successfully? (4) Are students persisting in pursuing their academic goals? Common measures of evaluation include persistence from term to term, the ratio of credit hours earned to those attempted, and grade point average. The academic progress of underprepared students should be compared to that of students who are college-ready. If possible, underprepared students who complete a program of developmental education should also be compared to those who do not.

The first measure used to assess the effectiveness of developmental education programs is the developmental education course completion rate. Haeuser (1993) defined a course completion success rate at Anne Arundel Community College in Maryland as the percentage of students who earned passing grades of C or higher. Developmental education course completion success rates from fall 1990 were compared to overall divisional success rates. Seventy-three percent of students enrolled in developmental English successfully completed their coursework, whereas the overall success rate for the English division was 71 percent. The course completion success rate for students enrolled in developmental math was 53 percent, and the overall success rate for the math division was 58 percent. Over half of the students enrolled in developmental education courses, therefore, successfully completed their developmental education coursework.

The effectiveness of developmental education programs is also assessed in terms of student movement from developmental education to college-level courses. Faculty and staff who work with underprepared students believe that success in developmental education courses improves student motivation and enhances self-confidence so that students are likely to enroll in college-level courses. Seybert and Soltz (1992) examined the course-taking patterns of students who enrolled in at least one developmental education course at Johnson County Community College in Kansas. The developmental education students included in the study completed an average of twenty credit hours at the college. More than 70 percent of the students enrolled for at least one semester after completing a developmental education course. The authors concluded, "A large majority of students in developmental courses enroll in additional coursework at the college, much of it at college level" (p. 33).

The third measure used to assess the effectiveness of developmental education programs is the successful completion of college-level coursework. Schoenecker, Bollman, and Evens (1996) examined developmental education outcomes for twenty-one community colleges in Minnesota. Performance measures, including the ratio of credits earned to credits attempted and grade point average, were examined in the content areas of reading, writing, and math. At a majority of the colleges, students who completed developmental education programs had significantly higher ratios of credits earned to credits attempted than underprepared students who chose not to enroll in developmental education. The study also revealed that students who completed developmental education programs earned significantly higher GPAs than underprepared students who opted not to enroll in developmental education courses. At a majority of colleges, students who completed developmental programs also performed as well as or better than college-ready students. This study, therefore, suggests that students who successfully complete a developmental education program succeed in college-level coursework as well.

The final measure used to assess the effectiveness of developmental education programs is student persistence. The Office of Institutional Planning and Research at Sinclair Community College in Ohio analyzed the progress of developmental education students over a three-year period (Sinclair Community College, 1995). Persistence was measured by an overall retention rate. The study revealed that 51 percent of students who completed all of their developmental education courses were still enrolled at the college after three years. The overall retention rate for college-ready students was 43 percent, whereas underprepared students who took some developmental education courses had a retention rate of 36 percent and underprepared students who chose not to enroll in a developmental education program had a rate of 31 percent. Thus, completion of a developmental education program was positively related to student persistence in this study.

The research studies described above provide important information on ways to measure effectiveness. However, assessing student progress and outcomes is just the beginning of evaluation. Each college must then determine acceptable and appropriate standards to indicate effectiveness. After gathering and analyzing data, a college will usually find that not all underprepared students are succeeding. It must then decide if changes can be made to increase the number of students completing developmental education courses and to raise the level of performance and the persistence rates of students who move on to college-level courses. Expanding research to include policy issues will provide further information for decision making.

Evaluating Policies

The mission of the community college is directly linked to providing access to all students who can benefit and to enhancing opportunities for students to accomplish their academic and career goals. Policies governing developmental education programs must achieve a balance between maintaining academic standards and ensuring access. These policies must be designed to facilitate student success without lowering the quality of the academic programs and without limiting access to students who can benefit from the educational offerings of the college. Continuous examination and monitoring of such policies results in more effective programs. Policies to be examined include placement, the timing of remediation, and enrollment in college-level courses. In addition, community colleges should look at varying policies according to the extent of deficiency (reading, writing, and math deficiency).

The survey of colleges and universities by the National Center for Education Statistics reported that "about three-quarters of the institutions indicated that remedial courses were required for students needing remediation. Public 2-year institutions required students to enroll in remedial courses less often than did public or private 4-year institutions" (USDE, 1996, p. 18). Yet the community college research literature confirms that mandatory placement in developmental courses is related to some measure of student success. In a study of developmental education at colleges and universities, Boylan, Bliss, and Bonham (1997) found that students enrolled in developmental education courses at two-year colleges where placement was mandatory were more likely to pass those courses than students enrolled in similar courses where placement was voluntary.

A study at the College of Lake County, a comprehensive community college in the northern suburbs of Chicago, found more striking results (Weissman, Silk, and Bulakowski, 1997). For the study, 1,226 college-ready students were compared to 239 underprepared students who had remediated and to 179 underprepared students who had not. After tracking the students for two years, from the fall semester of 1992 through the fall semester of 1994, the researchers found that the college-level students had earned an average GPA of 2.44, the students who had remediated earned an average GPA of 2.17, and the underprepared students who had not remediated earned an average GPA of 1.52. These grades were for college-level courses only, and the differences were found to be statistically significant. Although the average GPA for students who had remediated was not as high as that of college-ready students, the study did reveal that the students who had remediated performed at above a C average in their college-level courses. The students who had remediated also persisted at rates similar to those of college-ready students and completed their courses at rates similar to those of college-ready students. Underprepared students who did not remediate had low persistence rates and completed only 32 percent of the courses that they attempted. These results support a policy of mandatory placement.

The timing of remediation is another policy question to be addressed in evaluating the effectiveness of a developmental education program. Washtenaw Community College in Michigan conducted a study of 2,028 college-ready students and 1,254 underprepared students who entered the college in the fall of 1991 and the fall of 1992 (Campbell and Blakey, 1996). The researchers reported that completing developmental education courses during the first year of enrollment increased persistence, especially for those students least prepared for college-level courses.

The College of Lake County study (Weissman, Silk, and Bulakowski, 1997) reported somewhat different results. Initially, underprepared students who remediated in their first or second term of enrollment persisted at higher rates than students who remediated after their first year of enrollment. However, within a year after initial enrollment, the students in the study were exhibiting patterns of stopping out and returning to college. Although the results were not statistically significant, the students in the College of Lake County study who remediated within the first two academic terms of enrollment on average attempted more credit hours, earned more credit hours, and had higher GPAs than the underprepared students who remediated after their second term. The study also found that students who took developmental education courses during their first term of enrollment remediated at a much higher rate than students who did not attempt any developmental education courses during their first semester. The findings of these studies support a policy of requiring underprepared students to begin their developmental education courses on initial enrollment.

Colleges vary in their policies about students taking college-level courses while they are enrolled in developmental education courses. The National Center for Education Statistics survey found that "about two-thirds of institutions placed some restrictions on the regular academic courses that students could take while they were enrolled in remedial courses; about one-third of institutions did not place any restrictions on regular academic courses. Only 2 percent of institutions did not allow students to take any regular academic courses while they were taking remedial courses" (USDE, 1996, p. 20). Given community colleges' commitment to open-door admissions, it is essential for institutions to formulate clear policies concerning course enrollment for underprepared students. These policies should be grounded in research and should promote successful student outcomes.

A study by Castator and Tollefson examined the grades that eight thousand students at a Midwestern community college earned in college-level classes. Four groups of students were included in the analysis: college-ready students, underprepared students, underprepared students who had remediated prior to enrollment in college-level classes, and underprepared students who were concurrently enrolled in developmental education and college-level classes. The researchers discovered that underprepared students did not perform as well as students in the other groups. Underprepared students who had remediated or were concurrently enrolled in developmental education and college-level classes earned grades comparable to those of college-ready students. The authors concluded, "These findings strongly support the formulation of intrusive policies that require underprepared students to complete their developmental course work prior to or concurrently with enrollment in college-level courses" (Castator and Tollefson, 1996, p. 179).

A review of the research literature thus far suggests that the following policies lead to higher levels of performance and persistence for underprepared students.

- Underprepared students should be required to enroll in a program of developmental education.
- Underprepared students should be required to begin their developmental education program on initial enrollment.
- Underprepared students should be allowed to enroll in college-level courses before completing their developmental education programs as long as they are simultaneously working on remediation.

The question remains, Should these policies vary according to the extent of deficiency? Should students who are deficient in only one area be required to follow the same policies as those who are underprepared in reading, writing, and math? Two research studies shed some light on these policy questions.

The College of Lake County study (Weissman, Silk, and Bulakowski, 1997) found a significant relationship between the extent of student deficiency and the rate of remediation. Students underprepared in math only had the highest rate of remediation, followed by students who were language deficient (reading and/or writing). Triple deficient students (reading, writing, and math) were the least successful in remediating. In addition, students who were math deficient only had a higher average ratio of credit hours earned to credit hours attempted and a higher average GPA than students who were language deficient and triple deficient. Students who were triple deficient remediated at the lowest rate and had the lowest rate of persistence. These results were echoed by the Castator and Tollefson study (1996). This study found that students underprepared in reading and writing did not perform as well in college-level classes as students underprepared in math. These results point to the formulation of the following policy.

- Students underprepared in reading and writing and students underprepared in reading, writing, and math should be required to focus on their developmental education program before beginning college-level courses.

Conclusion

Community colleges are continually challenged about their mission of providing access to educational opportunities to all who can benefit. External forces demand accountability and results. The performance-based funding initiative sweeping the United States means that community colleges must be prepared to prove that the programs and policies they have established improve students' chances to succeed and achieve their academic goals.

Developmental education has long been a part of the community college mission and will continue to be an essential component of the offerings as long as community colleges pursue an open-door policy. However, admitting students to colleges does not mean that they should be allowed to sink or swim on their own. Colleges have a responsibility to institute programs and policies that promote student success. These programs and policies must achieve a balance between quality and access. They must be designed to help students achieve their goals without lowering the quality of the academic programs and without limiting access to educational offerings.

Continual monitoring and evaluation of developmental education programs are critical. Without evaluation, it is impossible to tell what is working and what is not. Evaluation must lead to decision making about changes that can be made to raise levels of student performance. Expanding assessment to include policy issues will provide further information for decision making. An evaluation process should address two questions: Are students succeeding? What policies contribute to student success?

The results from this review of the research literature support the following policies for community college developmental education programs.

- Underprepared students should be required to enroll in a program of developmental education.
- Underprepared students should be required to begin their developmental education program on initial enrollment.
- Underprepared students should be allowed to enroll in college-level courses before completing their developmental education programs as long as they are simultaneously working on remediation.

- Students underprepared in reading and writing and students underprepared in reading, writing, and math should be required to focus on their developmental education program before beginning college-level courses.

These policies are recommended to achieve maximum effectiveness, enhance student success, and balance access and quality.

References

Boylan, H. R., Bliss, L. B., and Bonham, B. S. "Program Components and Their Relationship to Student Performance." *Journal of Developmental Education*, 1997, *20* (3), 2–8.

Boylan, H. R., Bonham, B. S., and Bliss, L. B. "Characteristic Components of Developmental Programs." *Research in Developmental Education*, 1994, *11* (1).

Campbell, J. W., and Blakey, L. S. "Assessing the Impact of Early Remediation in the Persistence and Performance of Underprepared Community College Students." Paper presented at the Annual Forum of the Association of Institutional Research, Albuquerque, N.Mex., May 1996.

Castator, M. M., and Tollefson, N. "Underprepared Students and the College Curriculum: Identifying High-Risk Courses." *Journal of Applied Research in the Community College*, 1996, *3* (2), 179–200.

Haeuser, P. N. *Public Accountability and Developmental (Remedial) Education.* Arnold, Md.: Anne Arundel Community College, Office of Planning and Research, 1993. (ED 356 003)

Keimig, R. T. *Raising Academic Standards: A Guide to Learning Improvement.* ASHE-ERIC Higher Education Research Report 4. Washington, D.C.: Association for the Study of Higher Education, 1983.

Schoenecker, C., Bollman, L., and Evens, J. *Developmental Education Outcomes at Minnesota Community Colleges.* Paper presented at the Annual Forum of the Association of Institutional Research, Albuquerque, N.Mex., May 1996.

Seybert, J., and Soltz, D. F. *Assessing the Outcomes of Developmental Courses at Johnson County Community College.* Overland Park, Kans.: Johnson County Community College, Office of Institutional Research, 1992. (ED 349 052)

Sinclair Community College, Office of Institutional Planning and Research. "The Impact of Developmental Education on Student Progress: A Three Year Longitudinal Analysis." Paper presented at the Annual Forum of the Association of Institutional Research, Boston, Mass., May 1995.

U.S. Department of Education, National Center for Education Statistics. *Remedial Education at Higher Education Institutions in Fall 1995.* Washington, D.C.: U.S. Government Printing Office, 1996.

Weissman, J., Silk, E., and Bulakowski, C. "Assessing Developmental Education Policies." *Research in Higher Education*, 1997, *38* (2), 187–200.

Julie Weissman is director of institutional research and planning at the College of Lake County, Grayslake, Illinois.

Carole Bulakowski is assistant vice president of educational affairs at the College of Lake County, Grayslake, Illinois.

Marci K. Jumisko is research associate in institutional research and planning at the College of Lake County, Grayslake, Illinois.

This chapter discusses the requirements and limitations imposed by federal legislation that affects loans, grants, and work opportunities as they apply to students who need remedial/developmental coursework. Special note is made of financial aid considerations regarding students studying English as a second language and disabled students who need remediation.

Financial Aid and the Developmental Student

Michael B. Goldstein

Discussions about how best to serve the remedial or developmental student usually, and quite properly, center on the student's educational needs. Providing the right kind of learning opportunity in the right setting is, of course, essential to student success. But if a student cannot afford access to the appropriate learning services, the most carefully crafted program will be of no benefit. The federal government, through the student assistance programs established under the Higher Education Act of 1965 (the HEA) and its successor laws, has created a financial support system that is intended to ensure that no individual is denied access to a postsecondary education. These programs, commonly referred to as the Title IV programs for the portion of the HEA in which they are found, provide loans, grants, and work opportunities to a substantial majority of college students (20 U.S.C. Secs. 1070–1099).

Also involved is the Americans with Disabilities Act (the ADA), which requires "reasonable accommodation" to the special needs of the disabled to allow them to fully participate in a school's program. The ADA essentially parallels section 504 of the Rehabilitation Act of 1973, which provides that "no otherwise qualified individual . . . with a disability . . . shall, solely by reason of his or her disability, be excluded from the participation in, be denied the benefits of, or be subjected to discrimination under any program or activity receiving federal financial assistance." In this chapter, ADA will be used to

Assistance in preparing this chapter was provided by member Mary Qualiana, professional staff member Robin Minor, and law clerk Sean O'Connor at the law firm of Dow, Lohnes & Albertson, pllc.

denote the requirements of both laws. Also to be discussed is the Civil Rights Act of 1963, which affects the participation of developmental students in ways quite different from those of the ADA.

This chapter is intended neither to provide campus counsel with a treatise on the legal issues inherent in the conflict between federal laws, nor to offer an experienced student aid administrator specific guidance in the management of Title IV programs. (For the former, the reader is urged to examine Barber, 1996.) Financial aid administrators are commended to take advantage of the professional education programs offered by the National Association of Student Financial Aid Administrators and state and regional financial aid administrator organizations, in which these issues are increasingly being raised and discussed.

"Regular" Remedial/Developmental Instruction, Special Conditions, and Relevant Laws

A number of potential problems make the financial aid picture for the developmental student a complex one. A student may need remediation before being able to handle the coursework of a degree program; a disabled student may not be able to enroll in enough courses at a single time to maintain half-time enrollment; a student with a learning disability might not keep up with the standard of academic progress established by the institution; or a student may need ESL instruction in order to benefit from regular college-level coursework. All of these are common enough situations, but in each case accommodating to the student's needs may also result in denying that student access to the financial assistance to which he or she would otherwise be entitled. Can a student who is afforded access but denied the resources to take advantage of that access be truly considered "reasonably accommodated?" Current law at times seems to compel such an outcome. Only with the combined effort of several parts of an institution can this conundrum be resolved in a way that is both fair to the student and consistent with the requirements of law.

To participate in the Title IV programs, a student must be *regularly admitted* into a program of study leading to a *recognized degree or certificate* (34 C.F.R. Sec. 668.32 (1996)); must be able to complete the academic program within one and one-half times its expected length of time (34 C.F.R. Sec. 668.16 (1996)); and must be making *satisfactory academic progress* toward the credential (see generally 34 C.F.R. Part 668). If the student needs a loan to meet his or her college costs and expenses, he or she has to be attending on at least a half-time basis (34 C.F.R. Sec. 668.32 (1996)).

Conditions and Limitations of Financial Aid for Remedial Coursework

Generally, for purposes of federal financial aid, remedial courses count toward enrollment hours whether they are officially credit bearing, reduced credit, or noncredit courses toward the degree within the school (34 C.F.R. Sec. 668.20

(1996)). Further, students who are accepted contingent on completing remedial coursework are eligible for a full year of Federal Family Education Loan Program (FFEL) or Direct Loan funding before taking regular degree classes (34 C.F.R. 668.32 (1996)). Limits on funding remedial coursework exist where the proposed courses will still not adequately prepare the student to enter regular degree classes after one year, or where the classes are determined (by the state, regional accrediting organization, or institution) to be below the secondary level, although an exception is made for English as a second language (ESL) courses, discussed later in this chapter (34 C.F.R. Sec. 668.20).

Although the inclusion of remedial courses for financial aid enrollment purposes may allow a student to receive a more appropriate level of immediate, short-term aid, it may also cause the student to reach the aggregate cap on aid before completing all degree requirements. For example, under the federal Perkins loan guidelines, at a school participating in the Expanded Lending Option program, full-time students may borrow $4,000 annually, but are capped at a total aggregate amount of $8,000 until they have completed two years of a program leading to a bachelor's degree (34 C.F.R. Sec. 674.7 (1996)). Thus, if students need to take a few remedial courses during their first two years, they may not complete two years of degree credit within two academic years and, borrowing at the maximum amount, will have reached the cap prematurely. But once they complete the two years of degree credit, their aggregate cap increases to $20,000.

The restrictions on remedial coursework were enacted to limit the amount of federal funds appropriated for the support of postsecondary education from being used for instruction at less than that level. In other words, Title IV support should be for college-level work, not for support for the high school (or earlier) education that a student may have failed to receive or was denied.

To receive Title IV program assistance, the HEA requires that a student demonstrate that he or she is "maintaining satisfactory progress in the course of study the student is pursuing" in accordance with the specific requirements of the statute (20 U.S.C. Sec. 1091(a)(2)). The HEA goes on to define satisfactory academic progress as "a cumulative C average, or its equivalent, or academic standing consistent with the requirements for graduation, as determined by the institution, at the end of the second such academic year" (20 U.S.C. Sec. 1091(c)(1)(B)).

The Department of Education has promulgated extensive regulations governing the definition of satisfactory academic progress. These regulations are designed to prevent institutions from keeping students enrolled just to collect their tuition, where it is clear that the student is not actually progressing toward a degree or certificate. From a general public policy perspective, that is not an unreasonable position.

The Disabled Student

The student who requires remediation may or may not have a disability that would entitle him or her to accommodation under the ADA. A student who has learning disabilities that require special education services is clearly within the scope of the ADA (see C.F.R.Sec. 104.3(j)(2)(ii)). But for those who need such support because of an inadequate K–12 experience, the ADA does not come into play, and the obligation of the institution to admit and support the student is essentially a function of state law. That is, if an institution is required to be an "open access" institution, then a necessary element of that public policy is the need to provide academic support to students who arrive without adequate preparation. But if the institution fails to give adequate remediation, *and* the student is not disabled, there is no ADA violation. Students are granted special rights under the ADA when the need for remediation is the result of a disability; students whose remediation need is caused by a lack of secondary school preparation have no such rights. This has led to an uncomfortably high number of cases in which a student "discovers" a disability after having difficulty with his or her education. Although this is a topic unto itself, for the purposes of this chapter we are assuming that claimed disabilities are real and provable.

Remediation and Discrimination

This is not to say that the student who requires remediation but is not disabled is without rights. If a student requiring remediation can demonstrate that the failure to provide such service falls unevenly on particular racial or ethnic groups, there may be a violation of the Civil Rights Act (42 U.S.C. Sec 2000d) and the regulations of the Department of Education forbidding discrimination on the basis of race or ethnicity (34 C.F.R. Sec. 100.3(a)). This is a serious allegation, and one that can prompt an investigation by the Department of Education's Office for Civil Rights. Once a student alleges a civil rights violation, the Office for Civil Rights takes over the investigation; the complaining student has no further obligation, and does not even have to hire a private attorney. Office for Civil Rights investigations are usually thorough and often quite lengthy. The penalty for a serious violation by an institution can be the loss of eligibility to participate in any federal assistance programs, including the Title IV programs (34 C.F.R. Sec. 100.8). Since such an outcome would be disastrous for virtually any institution, Office for Civil Rights investigations are taken very seriously. Fortunately, this is now fairly well-established territory, and where unintended racial discrimination is found, the outcome is uniformly remedial rather than punitive.

Intentionally discriminating against students on the basis of race or ethnicity is, of course, a far more serious matter. For the purposes of this chapter, it is assumed that such intentional discrimination is not occurring. However, the courts have become increasingly concerned over what has come to be termed "reverse discrimination," in which students in one racial or ethnic group are given advantages over others in the name of making redress for prior discrimination against the former group. Although this is not directly at issue in dealing with developmental students, it is certainly possible to craft an institutional financial assistance program or administer the Title IV programs in such a way as to create the inference of such discrimination. A line of court cases has now emerged that requires an institution to show that financial assistance policies favoring one racial or ethnic group over another are narrowly designed to eliminate the effects of *presently existing* discrimination, rather than to redress the lingering shadows of prior discrimination, even if those "shadows" have had the effect of depressing minority enrollment at the institution.

For example, in *Podberesky v. Kirwan*, 38 F.3d 147 (4th Cir. 1994), the U.S. Court of Appeals struck down a university scholarship program designed to support African American students on the basis that the university had failed to demonstrate that the program was designed to eliminate the effects of presently existing discrimination. The Supreme Court declined to hear an appeal of the case. In crafting financial assistance for developmental students, an institution must be extremely careful to focus the program on the developmental needs of the students *independently* of race or ethnicity. If a program so crafted happens to benefit more students of one ethnic or racial group than another, that is a side effect that is independent of the students' race or ethnicity. But if race or ethnicity are among the bases for eligibility for the additional financial assistance, the strict tests established under recent case law come into play.

ESL Students and Financial Aid

Financial aid for ESL students is a special issue that requires campus administrators to distinguish between "remedial" and "stand alone" ESL programs, as stated in section 401(c)(2) of the HEA: "Nothing in this section shall exclude from eligibility courses of study which are non-credit or remedial in nature (including courses in English language instruction) which are determined by the institution to be necessary to help the student be prepared for the pursuit of a first undergraduate baccalaureate degree or certificate or, in the case of courses in English language instruction, to be necessary to enable the student to utilize already existing knowledge, training, or skills" (Goldstein and Blackmum, 1995, p. 1).

This recent addition to the HEA allows students who take ESL courses to receive federal financial aid in two quite different situations. The first situation considers ESL courses to be "remedial" in the sense that they are not college-level coursework but are a component of a degree, certificate, or diploma program in which the student is enrolled at the college. In this instance, the college must document that the student already meets regular admission standards and needs the remediation to improve English language skills. The ESL courses may be noncredit or reduced credit. They must also be counted in determining the student's enrollment status, and the student must be held to the academic progress standards of the institution. The second situation allows students to be eligible to receive Pell grants if they enroll in "stand-alone" ESL programs that provide the English language instruction necessary to "make use of '*already existing* knowledge, training, or skills' " (Goldstein and Blackmum, 1995, p. 2). A limitation on this second situation is that only Pell grants are available to students in stand-alone ESL programs, unlike federal financial aid available to students in ESL programs that are considered remedial. A stand-alone ESL program can consist solely of ESL instruction. Preparation for employment need not be a goal of the stand-alone ESL program in order for the student to be eligible for Pell grants. And if an ESL program contains a substantial employment training component along with ESL instruction, then it is considered remedial ESL. Campus administrators need to be aware of the distinctions between these two types of ESL instruction and the resulting differences in the way federal student aid funds may be used. If questions concerning the purpose and structure of the ESL program and student admission and enrollment in degree or certificate programs are not carefully considered and documented, "the institution may find itself subject to significant potential liability for the financial aid disbursed to students enrolled in its ESL programs" (Goldstein and Blackmum, 1995, p. 2).

Concluding Thoughts

The obligation to accommodate the needs of the developmental student is a matter of fundamental fairness as well as good public policy. It is also an area that is rife with a variety of federal laws that seek to protect the rights of individuals *and* the integrity of federal funds. At times, these interests come into conflict, as they do most clearly in seeking to accommodate to the financial assistance needs of students with disabilities. This conflict does not mean that the needs of such students cannot be met. It does mean that in meeting those needs the current state of the law has to be carefully considered. That, in turn, means that in crafting and administering such programs there must be close communication and collaboration between the responsible academic officers, the institution's financial aid administrator, and campus counsel. With that interaction, the issues discussed above are manageable, and the problems explored avoidable. Without that, there is the real potential for disaster.

References

Barber, C. K. "Waivers of Academic Progress Requirements for Federal Financial Aid: A Reasonable Accommodation for Students with Learning Disabilities?" *Journal of College and University Law,* 1996, 2 (23), 231–253.

Goldstein, M. B., and Blackmum, E. V. *Managing Federal Student Aid for Students Enrolled in English as a Second Language Courses and Programs.* Notes from AACC Counsel. Washington, D.C.: American Association of Community Colleges, August 1995.

MICHAEL B. GOLDSTEIN *is a member of the Washington, D.C., law firm of Dow, Lohnes & Albertson, pllc.*

This chapter provides an annotated bibliography of materials from the ERIC system that highlight major policy issues in providing remedial/developmental education within higher education as well as studies that have measured the effectiveness of different policies.

Sources and Information About Remedial/Developmental Education Programs

Kristen J. McKinney

The following ERIC publications provide information on major policy issues involved in delivering remedial/developmental education and highlight some of the major controversies in providing remedial/developmental education at community colleges, including questions of the role and mission of the community college, the testing and placement of students who need remediation, the role remediation plays in providing access to higher education by underrepresented groups, and the need for institutions to be accountable for the remedial/developmental education they provide. The publications also present several state and local studies that have measured the effectiveness of those policies and in several cases compare the success of students who take remedial/developmental classes with students who do not require remediation.

Most ERIC documents (publications with ED numbers) can be viewed on microfiche at over nine hundred libraries worldwide. In addition, most may be ordered on microfiche or on paper from the ERIC Document Reproduction Service (EDRS) by calling (800) 443-ERIC. Journal articles are not available from EDRS, but they can be acquired through regular library channels or purchased from one of the following article reproduction services: Carl Uncover: [http://www.carl.org/uncover/], <uncover@carl.org>, (800) 787–7979; UMI: <orders@infostore.com>, (800) 248–0360; or ISI: <tga@isinet.com>, (800) 523–1850.

Policies on Remedial/Developmental Education

These documents provide information about how remedial programs are instituted in a variety of settings, discuss the policy issues involved in implementation, and address how changes in developmental education policy in one sector can affect other sectors of higher education.

Maryland Higher Education Commission. *A Study of Remedial Education at Maryland Public Campuses.* Annapolis: Maryland Higher Education Commission, 1996.

This report outlines the results from a statewide survey of remedial education programs at Maryland public higher education institutions. The study examined the number and type of students who require remediation; the policies, instruments, and standards that are used to determine student placement in and completion of remedial courses; the kinds of remedial courses and activities offered; the success of remedial students and the evaluation of remedial programs; staffing for remedial courses; the cost of remedial education; and the sources from which it is funded. The majority of the results are presented for each college in the system. In addition, analyses by student gender, ethnicity, and age categories, as well as higher education sector (two- or four-year) are also included. The report concludes with a discussion of the policy questions that arise from the findings. The forty-five-page report includes twenty-three tables and a copy of the survey instrument.

Patricia N. Haeuser. *Public Accountability and Developmental Education.* Arnold, Md.: Anne Arundel Community College, Office of Planning and Research, 1993. (ED 356 003)

Despite their vital role in open-access, two-year colleges, remedial education efforts have increasingly come under attack by legislators and the public, who view such programs as duplicating the appropriate function of high schools and who believe that limited state resources should be devoted to more prestigious programs. For a college to effectively defend such a program, it is crucial that it be linked to the institution's mission. In addition, a college's accountability analysis of its remedial programs should focus on the program population, rather than on a description of the program. At Anne Arundel Community College in Arnold, Maryland, a comparison of remedial students with the general student population revealed that minority students, transfer-oriented students, and full-timers were all overrepresented among remedial students. These data can help the college convince a skeptical public that its remedial programs are improving retention rates for minority students and full-time, transfer-oriented students, both populations the programs were intended to help. Appropriate outcomes assessments are also vital in demonstrating a program's importance. At Anne Arundel Community College, outcomes measures have shown that (1) over half of remedial students successfully complete developmental courses; (2) first-time remedial students have higher fall-to-spring retention rates than first-time students as a whole; and (3) most remedial English students successfully complete subsequent college-level courses. Finally, cost analyses can help demonstrate a program's value. At Anne Arundel Community College, such analyses have shown that developmental courses have lower costs per student than the average general education course.

California Community Colleges. *Scope, Implications, and Impact: The Academic Senate for California Community Colleges' Response to the Proposed CSU Policy to Eliminate Remedial Education for Entering Undergraduate Students.* Sacramento: Academic Senate for California Community Colleges, 1995. (ED 395 627)

In November 1994 the California State University (CSU) system developed a proposal to eliminate remedial education for entering undergraduate students, offering this proposal as a solution to raise the system's standards. However, the CSU system presented no research showing evidence of the problem that the proposal is intended to solve. Further, while the CSU presumably holds K–12 and community colleges accountable for the availability of students prepared to enter college-level English and math, the system has not held itself responsible for accurately determining the status of enrolled students. Placement tests used by the CSU system to determine students in need of remediation do not reflect state standards set for English and mathematics curricula, with only approximately one-third of the students taking the English and approximately one-fourth of the students taking the mathematics placement test in 1993 performing at college-ready levels. It is uncertain whether the system has the authority to unilaterally make such a programming decision, and the process was undertaken without coordination with other segments of public education in California. Finally, implementation of the proposal would have a considerable effect on the number of students seeking remedial coursework at the community colleges, placing further strain on resources at the colleges and possibly affecting diversity at CSU campuses. Recommendations for addressing these issues are included. The report is sixteen pages long.

Anita Colby and Ron Opp. *Controversies Surrounding Developmental Education in the Community College.* ERIC Digest. Los Angeles: ERIC Clearinghouse for Junior Colleges, 1987. (ED 286 557)

In this ERIC *Digest,* the authors present the following common criticisms about large-scale community college involvement in developmental education and counter each of them: (1) Community colleges are the wrong places to provide developmental education. (2) Developmental education should be the responsibility of a separate instructional division, not the responsibility of instructors in the collegiate curricula. (3) Community college faculty members do not know how to teach literacy. (4) There is insufficient articulation between community colleges and secondary schools. (5) Placement and diagnostic tests for students in developmental education are not valid. The authors conclude that the arguments against the provision of developmental education in the community colleges are based on a lack of understanding of the nature and goals of developmental programs and that developmental education is at the heart of the open-door philosophy.

Abraham A. Ansley. "They Came to College? A Remedial/Developmental Profile of First-Time Freshmen in SREB States." *Issues in Higher Education,* 1991, *25.* (ED 333 783)

This paper reports the results of a survey of remedial programs at public and private colleges and universities in the southern region of the United States and highlights remedial education patterns by state, race, and gender. Responses were received from 606 of the 826 institutions surveyed (73 percent). Among the report's findings are the following: (1) Remedial enrollment at private institutions in the region (32 percent) is only slightly lower than the rate at public institutions (36 percent). (2) States that have mandatory testing and placement policies tend to have higher percentages of freshmen in remedial courses. (3) Remedial enrollment rates for Blacks and Hispanics are consistently one and one-half to two times that of White students. (4) Thirty-nine percent of entering freshmen need remedial assistance in mathematics. (5) Remedial enrollment at most public and private institutions has increased since 1984; two-year colleges had the largest increase, and doctoral institutions the least, but an average of 25 percent of freshmen at doctoral institutions needed at least one remedial course. The report explores implications of high levels of underpreparation present among Black and Hispanic students, as well as ethical questions raised by college-level remedial programs. It is suggested that colleges and universities closely examine their expectations for remedial students and the institution's willingness to invest in the quality of program necessary to get students ready for full-time college work.

E. A. Morante. "Selecting Tests and Placing Students." *Journal of Developmental Education,* 1989, *13* (2), 2–4, 6.

This article advocates the testing and placement of incoming college students, arguing that students need access to information on their personal attributes and institutional options. The author identifies criteria to be considered in selecting placement tests and making placement decisions. Included are suggestions for creating a systematic placement process.

R. E. Hughes and C. H. Nelson. "Placement Scores and Placement Practices: An Empirical Analysis." *Community College Review,* 1991, *19* (1), 42–46.

This analysis assesses the accuracy of Riverside Community College's entry-level assessment and placement practice, correlating reading and language assessment scores with grades in freshman composition and student demographics. The authors conclude that ASSET (Assessment of Student Skills for Entry Transfer) test scores alone were not strong predictors of student success and that other data sources should be considered as well.

Michigan State Board of Education. *A Survey of Student Assessment and Developmental Education in Michigan's Public Community Colleges. Executive Summary. Second State Survey.* Lansing: Michigan State Board of Education, 1990. (ED 320 624)

In 1989 a study was conducted of the status of student assessment and developmental education in Michigan's twenty-nine public community colleges and three public four-year colleges that serve in a community college capacity. The study sought to determine (1) the number of community college students in need of and actually enrolled in developmental services in reading, writing, math computation, algebra, and other areas; (2) policies on developmental education and course credit; (3) the types of students who are assessed, the tests used, policies related to mandatory testing and placement, and cutoff scores for placement in remedial courses; (4) the developmental populations colleges are prepared to accommodate; (5) courses in the developmental curriculum and skill areas addressed; (6) types of support services provided; (7) class times and locations; (8) the job titles, experience, and turnover rates of developmental faculty; (9) the existence of professional development programs to prepare staff to work with underprepared students; (10) information on cooperative programs with elementary and secondary schools, community organizations, and business and industry; (11) the scope of evaluation efforts; and (12) strengths and weaknesses in developmental efforts. Based on study findings, a series of recommendations were developed for implementation by the board of education, the governor, and the state legislature. The survey instrument is included.

Effectiveness of Developmental Programs

These documents focus on the effectiveness of developmental programs and how they can be evaluated.

Julie Weissman and others. *Assessing Developmental Education Through Student Tracking.* AIR Annual Forum Paper. Tallahassee: Association for Institutional Research, 1995. (ED 386 983)

The effectiveness of developmental education policies at a comprehensive community college was investigated using a new student tracking system. A sample of 1,644 students was tracked from fall 1992 until the end of the fall 1994 semester, 1,226 of whom evidenced basic skills and were eligible for college-level courses, and 418 of whom were classified as skill-deficient. After the fall 1994 semester, 179 skill-deficient students had not remediated and 239 had remediated. The college-level and skill-deficient students were compared on persistence and performance. Also examined were links between skill-deficient students' academic performance and their enrollment patterns in developmental education courses exclusively, college-level courses and remedial courses, and college-level courses only. Additional concerns were rates of remediation and types of problems (math only, language only, or both, and reading or writing deficiency, or both). Results support the following recommendations: skill-deficient students should be required to remediate on initial enrollment, and these students should be allowed to take college-level courses along with remedial studies, but language deficient and triple deficient students should be encouraged to finish remediation before beginning college-level courses. In conclusion, the results point to guidelines for designing or revising policies governing developmental education programs. The paper contains eleven references.

P. Hopper, R. Taylor, and P. Wolford. *Success Rate of Developmental vs. Nondevelopmental Students in Freshman College Level English.* Morristown, Tenn.: Walters State Community College, 1996.

This study compared the pass rates of developmental and nondevelopmental students in freshman English classes at Walters State Community College. Using chi-square analysis, the percentage of former developmental students who passed freshman English was compared to that of nondevelopmental students. Based on a review of student records, 817 students were categorized as either developmental or nondevelopmental, and the percentage who passed was calculated for each group. The passing rates for nondevelopmental students were significantly higher when all grades were evaluated. However, when course withdrawals and incompletes were excluded from consideration, there were no significant differences between the two groups. This nineteen-page report includes six references, two appendices, and three tables.

J. M. Pitts and W. G. White. *The Impact of Underprepared Students on Regular College Faculty.* Paper presented at the 2nd National Conference on Research in Developmental Education, Charlotte, N.C., Oct. 1996.

This document reports the results of a qualitative research study conducted at two open-admission universities in the South. Fourteen faculty members were interviewed to assess their experiences with underprepared students. Three major themes are presented: (1) basic problems and dilemmas associated with academic underpreparedness, (2) responses and coping strategies employed to deal with problems and dilemmas, and (3) opinions, values, and feelings relevant to salient issues. Among the fundamental problems and dilemmas are students' lack of basic knowledge and skill levels, as well as their lack of motivation and poor attitudes toward academic study. In addition, lack of resources and adequate administrative support were found to be problematic. Instructors' responses to these problems included changes in teaching behaviors, course content, and evaluation. The issues found to be most salient to instructors teaching underprepared students were the philosophy of open admissions and the role of developmental education, the instructors' own personal dilemmas, including feelings of role ambiguity and value conflicts, and discussion of prescriptive measures that should be taken to improve the quality of education. This twenty-eight-page paper includes fourteen references.

Louise M. Tomlinson. *Postsecondary Developmental Programs: A Traditional Agenda with New Imperatives.* ASHE-ERIC Higher Education Report 3. Washington, D.C.: ERIC Clearinghouse on Higher Education, 1989. (ED 316 076)

This report examines postsecondary developmental education for students denied regular admission to the institution. Addressed are such concerns as the evolution of developmental programs, the effect of developmental programs on the integrity of the academic institutions, and the future of postsecondary developmental programs. The report's seven sections discuss the following topics and subtopics: (1) the historical perspective of postsecondary developmental education (the evolution of developmental programs in the United States and the purpose, function, nature, definition, and ambiguities of such programs); (2) the rationale for developmental programs (new target population, projections, arguments on role and responsibility, learning deficiencies, experiential deficiencies, and standardized placement trends, such as those relying on SAT averages); (3) characteristics of postsecondary developmental programs (alternative structures, types of interventions, delivery modes, operational models, and the role of junior and senior colleges and universities); (4) exemplars and problems in the delivery of developmental services (profiles of two successful programs, factors of success), personnel, program design, general criticisms, and problems; (5) program evaluation (assessment of program evaluation, focus and findings, and evaluation designs and implications); (6) changes in education and the challenge to developmental curriculum (including a comparison of Sternberg on training intelligence, Feurstein on instrumental enrichment, and Lipman on philosophy in the classroom); and (7) policy and possibilities for future developmental programs (the role of the state in policy, training administrators and faculty, the prospective developmental student population, the general prosperity of programs, and developmental research).

KRISTEN J. MCKINNEY is a doctoral student in the Division of Higher Education, University of California at Los Angeles, and outreach coordinator for the ERIC Clearinghouse for Community Colleges.

INDEX

ORDERING INFORMATION

NEW DIRECTIONS FOR COMMUNITY COLLEGES is a series of paperback books that provides expert assistance to help community colleges meet the challenges of their distinctive and expanding educational mission. Books in the series are published quarterly in Spring, Summer, Fall, and Winter and are available for purchase by subscription and individually.

SUBSCRIPTIONS cost $55.00 for individuals (a savings of 37 percent over single-copy prices) and $98.00 for institutions, agencies, and libraries. Please do not send institutional checks for personal subscriptions. Standing orders are accepted. Prices subject to change. (For subscriptions outside of North America, add $7.00 for shipping via surface mail or $25.00 for air mail. Orders must be prepaid in U.S. dollars by check drawn on a U.S. bank or charged to VISA, MasterCard, or American Express.)

SINGLE COPIES cost $22.00 plus shipping (see below) when payment accompanies order. California, New Jersey, New York, and Washington, D.C., residents please include appropriate sales tax. Canadian residents add GST and any local taxes. Billed orders will be charged shipping and handling. No billed shipments to post office boxes. (Orders from outside North America must be prepaid in U.S. dollars by check drawn on a U.S. bank or charged to VISA, MasterCard, or American Express.)

SHIPPING (SINGLE COPIES ONLY): $30.00 and under, add 5.50; to $50.00 add $6.50; to $75.00, add $7.50; to $100.00, add $9.00; to $150.00, add $10.00.

DISCOUNTS for quantity orders are available. Please write to the address below for information.

ALL ORDERS must include either the name of an individual or an official purchase order number. Please submit your order as follows:
Subscriptions: specify series and year subscription is to begin
Single copies: include individual title code (such as CC82)

MAIL ORDERS TO:
Jossey-Bass Publishers
350 Sansome Street
San Francisco, California 94104–1342

PHONE subscription or single-copy orders toll-free at (888) 378–2537 or at (415) 433–1767 (toll call).

FAX orders toll-free to (800) 605–2665.

FOR SUBSCRIPTION SALES OUTSIDE OF THE UNITED STATES, contact any international subscription agency or Jossey-Bass directly.

OTHER TITLES AVAILABLE IN THE
NEW DIRECTIONS FOR COMMUNITY COLLEGES SERIES
Arthur M. Cohen, Editor-in-Chief
Florence B. Brawer, Associate Editor

UNITED STATES POSTAL SERVICE™

Statement of Ownership, Management, and Circulation
(Required by 39 USC 3685)

1. Publication Title	2. Publication Number	3. Filing Date
NEW DIRECTIONS FOR COMMUNITY COLLEGES	0 1 9 4 – 3 0 8 1	9/15/97

4. Issue Frequency	5. Number of Issues Published Annually	6. Annual Subscription Price
QUARTERLY	4	$55 – indiv. $98 – instit.

7. Complete Mailing Address of Known Office of Publication *(Not printer)* *(Street, city, county, state, and ZIP+4)*
350 SANSOME STREET
SAN FRANCISCO, CA   94104
(SAN FRANCISCO COUNTY)

Contact Person: ROGER HUNT
Telephone: 415 782 3232

8. Complete Mailing Address of Headquarters or General Business Office of Publisher *(Not printer)*
SAME AS ABOVE

9. Full Names and Complete Mailing Addresses of Publisher, Editor, and Managing Editor *(Do not leave blank)*

Publisher *(Name and complete mailing address)*
JOSSEY-BASS INC., PUBLISHERS
(ABOVE ADDRESS)

Editor *(Name and complete mailing address)*
ARTHUR COHEN, ERIC CLEARINGHOUSE FOR COMMUNITY CLGS.
SCHOOL OF EDUCATION, UCLA
3051 MOORE HALL, 405 HILGARD AVE.
LOS ANGELES, CA   90024-1521

Managing Editor *(Name and complete mailing address)*
NONE

10. Owner *(Do not leave blank. If the publication is owned by a corporation, give the name and address of the corporation immediately followed by the names and addresses of all stockholders owning or holding 1 percent or more of the total amount of stock. If not owned by a corporation, give the names and addresses of the individual owners. If owned by a partnership or other unincorporated firm, give its name and address as well as those of each individual owner. If the publication is published by a nonprofit organization, give its name and address.)*

Full Name	Complete Mailing Address
SIMON & SCHUSTER	P.O. BOX 1172
	ENGLEWOOD CLIFFS, NJ 07632-1172

11. Known Bondholders, Mortgagees, and Other Security Holders Owning or Holding 1 Percent or More of Total Amount of Bonds, Mortgages, or Other Securities. If none, check box ▶ ☐ None

Full Name	Complete Mailing Address
SAME AS ABOVE	SAME AS ABOVE

12. Tax Status *(For completion by nonprofit organizations authorized to mail at special rates)* *(Check one)*
The purpose, function, and nonprofit status of this organization and the exempt status for federal income tax purposes:
☐ Has Not Changed During Preceding 12 Months
☐ Has Changed During Preceding 12 Months *(Publisher must submit explanation of change with this statement)*

PS Form **3526**, September 1995   *(See Instructions on Reverse)*

---

13. Publication Title	14. Issue Date for Circulation Data Below
NEW DIRECTIONS FOR COMMUNITY COLLEGES	SUMMER 1997

15. Extent and Nature of Circulation		Average No. Copies Each Issue During Preceding 12 Months	Actual No. Copies of Single Issue Published Nearest to Filing Date
a. Total Number of Copies *(Net press run)*		1846	2063
b. Paid and/or Requested Circulation	(1) Sales Through Dealers and Carriers, Street Vendors, and Counter Sales *(Not mailed)*	110	34
	(2) Paid or Requested Mail Subscriptions *(Include advertiser's proof copies and exchange copies)*	803	810
c. Total Paid and/or Requested Circulation *(Sum of 15b(1) and 15b(2))* ▶		913	844
d. Free Distribution by Mail *(Samples, complimentary, and other free)*		0	0
e. Free Distribution Outside the Mail *(Carriers or other means)*		216	210
f. Total Free Distribution *(Sum of 15d and 15e)* ▶		216	210 *i*
g. Total Distribution *(Sum of 15c and 15f)* ▶		1129	1054
h. Copies not Distributed	(1) Office Use, Leftovers, Spoiled	717	1009
	(2) Returns from News Agents	0	0
i. Total *(Sum of 15g, 15h(1), and 15h(2))* ▶		1846	2063
Percent Paid and/or Requested Circulation *(15c / 15g x 100)*		81%	80%

16. Publication of Statement of Ownership
☒ Publication required. Will be printed in the **WINTER 1997** issue of this publication.
☐ Publication not required.

17. Signature and Title of Editor, Publisher, Business Manager, or Owner
Susan E. Lewis   SUSAN E. LEWIS   DIRECTOR OF PERIODICALS
Date: 9/18/97

I certify that all information furnished on this form is true and complete. I understand that anyone who furnishes false or misleading information on this form or who omits material or information requested on the form may be subject to criminal sanctions (including fines and imprisonment) and/or civil sanctions (including multiple damages and civil penalties).

Instructions to Publishers

1. Complete and file one copy of this form with your postmaster annually on or before October 1. Keep a copy of the completed form for your records.

2. In cases where the stockholder or security holder is a trustee, include in items 10 and 11 the name of the person or corporation for whom the trustee is acting. Also include the names and addresses of individuals who are stockholders who own or hold 1 percent or more of the total amount of bonds, mortgages, or other securities of the publishing corporation. In item 11, if none, check the box. Use blank sheets if more space is required.

3. Be sure to furnish all circulation information called for in item 15. Free circulation must be shown in items 15d, e, and f.

4. If the publication had second-class authorization as a general or requester publication, this Statement of Ownership, Management, and Circulation must be published; it must be printed in any issue in October or, if the publication is not published during October, the first issue printed after October.

5. In item 16, indicate the date of the issue in which this Statement of Ownership will be published.

6. Item 17 must be signed.

Failure to file or publish a statement of ownership may lead to suspension of second-class authorization.

PS Form **3526**, September 1995 *(Reverse)*